I0117681

Anonymus

Rules, Forms and Schedule of Fees issued by Irish Land

Commission, October 1881

Anonymus

Rules, Forms and Schedule of Fees issued by Irish Land Commission, October 1881

ISBN/EAN: 9783742806062

Manufactured in Europe, USA, Canada, Australia, Japa

Cover: Foto ©Suzi / pixelio.de

Manufactured and distributed by brebook publishing software (www.brebook.com)

Anonymus

Rules, Forms and Schedule of Fees issued by Irish Land

Commission, October 1881

LAND LAW (IRELAND) ACT, 1881 (RULES, FORMS, &c.).

COPY

OF

RULES, FORMS, AND SCHEDULE OF FEES

ISSUED BY THE

IRISH LAND COMMISSION.

LAND LAW (IRELAND) ACT, 1881.

RULES.

Saturday the 1st of October 1881.

It is this day ordered that the following general rules and orders shall from this date, until further order, take effect, and be in force in the Land Commission in relation to all proceedings held or taken under, and in pursuance of, the Land Law (Ireland) Act, 1881, or any part of any Act incorporated therewith. It is likewise ordered that such of the said rules and orders as are expressly or by manifest implication applicable to proceedings in the Civil Bill Court, under the said Act, or any part of any Act incorporated therewith, shall take effect and be in force in the several Civil Bill Courts in Ireland.

1. All rules and regulations of the late Commissioners of Church Temporalities in Ireland in force prior to the 13th day of September 1881, pursuant to the 8th section of the Irish Church Act, 1869, shall remain and continue in force and be applicable to all proceedings which shall be necessary in relation to the administration of Church Temporalities in Ireland until further order, as fully as if the Church Temporalities Commission were in existence.

2. All rules heretofore in existence in the Civil Bill Courts, inconsistent with the following general orders, so far as proceedings under the Land Law (Ireland) Act, 1881, hereinafter referred to as "The Act," or any part of any Act incorporated therewith are concerned, are hereby annulled, and all rules heretofore in existence in relation to appeals for the determination of any matter under the Act, or under the Landlord and Tenant (Ireland) Act, 1870, are hereby also annulled.

DEFINITIONS.

3. In the construction of these rules the word "Court" shall mean either the Civil Bill Court, or else the Land Commission, in case, at the option of the party, the matter has been originated in, or has been, by order, transferred to such Land Commission.

4. The word "order" shall include decree, award, ruling, and adjudication of the Court in any case.

5. The word "county" shall include county of a city and county of a town, and a riding of a county, where such county of a city, county of a town, or riding, is appointed for Civil Bill purposes.

83.   A   6. The

6. The expression "Clerk of the Peace" shall include the Clerk of the Crown and Peace.

7. The expression "Secretary of the Commission" shall include every person who for the time being shall discharge the duties of the Secretary of the Irish Land Commission.

8. In the computation of time for the purpose of these rules, the word "month" shall mean calendar month, and the period of a month shall not be extended by reason of any intervening holiday, but when the time limited is a week or fortnight, such week or fortnight shall be extended by any intervening holiday or holidays except Sundays.

9. Whenever the time limited expires on a Sunday, or other holiday, it shall be extended to the next open day.

10. "Holiday" shall, as regards the Land Commission, mean any day on which the offices of the Land Commission shall not be open, pursuant to the rules.

11. The several offices of the Land Commission shall be open throughout the year.

12. The offices of the Land Commission shall be open daily from ten o'clock, a.m., till four o'clock, p.m., except on Saturdays, when they shall close at one o'clock, p.m.

13. The Court of the Land Commission shall sit in the following places for the purpose of hearing appeals from the Civil Bill Courts, and of re-hearing cases tried by Sub-Commission; that is to say:—

In BELFAST, where the cases have been tried in -	Down. Antrim. Armagh. Monaghan.
In LONDONDERRY, where the cases have been tried in -	Londonderry. Donegal. Tyrone. Fermanagh.
In GALWAY, where the cases have been tried in -	Galway. Mayo. Roscommon.
In MULLINGAR, where the cases have been tried in	Leitrim. Sligo. Longford. Westmeath.
In LIMERICK, where the cases have been tried in -	Limerick. Clare. Tipperary.
In KILLARNEY, where the cases have been tried in	Kerry.
In CORK, where the cases have been tried in -	Cork. Waterford.
In DUBLIN, where the cases have been tried in -	Dublin. Wexford. Kilkenny. Carlow. Queen's County. King's County. Kildare. Wicklow. Meath. Louth. Cavan.

14. On consent of parties, or on special grounds, the Land Commission may direct an appeal or re-hearing to be heard elsewhere than as above.

15. The times for holding such sittings shall be duly notified.

ASSISTANT COMMISSIONERS.

Sub-Commissions.

16. Assistant Commissioners shall hold office until the 22nd August 1888, subject to the provisions of the Land Law (Ireland) Act, 1881. Barristers, solicitors, and persons possessing a practical acquaintance with the value of land in Ireland, shall be competent to be appointed to the office.

17. Sub-Commissions shall ordinarily consist of three Assistant Commissioners, but may consist of a greater or less number, and with or without a Commissioner, as the Commissioners may from time to time in any special case direct.

18. Each Sub-Commission shall act by virtue of an instrument of delegation under the Seal of the Land Commission, and shall possess the powers therein specified, subject to the right of the Land Commission to revoke, alter, or modify all powers so delegated.

19. The Sub-Commission shall hold its sittings in the court-houses of quarter sessions or petty sessions as its members shall find most suitable, having regard to the matters coming before them for their decision and the convenience of the parties, and they shall from time to time duly notify in such manner as they shall deem best the times and places of their sittings.

20. It shall be the duty of the Sub-Commission or of one or more of its members so far as practicable to visit in person the holding in any case in which they deem that such visit may conduce to a just decision.

21. If the Sub-Commission be not in attendance to hold a Court on the appointed day, the Clerk of the Peace, or his deputy, or principal assistant, may adjourn the Court for a reasonable time, and may do so from time to time until the Sub-Commission sits.

PROCEDURE.

22. Procedure under the Act shall not be by pleadings, but shall be by notices, as hereinafter directed. The Court may at all times amend notices, and may, if it think fit, extend the time prescribed by these rules for serving notices or doing any other act. All notices and affidavits shall be on paper of foolscap size, with proper margin for binding.

23. The first notice of application to the Court seeking its decision upon the question of the true value of a tenancy, fair rent, avoidance of lease, or any other question which the Court has jurisdiction to decide under the Act, shall be termed an originating notice.

24. Every originating notice shall designate the Court selected, either the Civil Bill Court or the Land Commission. It shall be first served on the opposite party, that is to say, on the landlord or tenant, or other person or persons sought to be bound by the decision of the Court, and forthwith after such service, or the last of such services, if more than one, two copies thereof shall be served on the Clerk of the Peace, or one copy on the Land Commission, according to the Court selected.

25. Whenever a notice is by these rules required to be served on the Clerk of the Peace, two copies thereof shall be so served in order to enable the duplicate to be transmitted as hereinafter directed.

26. The copy of an originating notice served on the Land Commission, or one of the copies served on the Clerk of the Peace, shall be endorsed with a statement of the time and mode of service of the party or parties served, and so soon as an originating notice has been served upon the Clerk of the Peace or the Land Commission, as the case may be, as well as upon the party or parties, the matter shall be deemed to be in Court as a case to be decided.

B3.　　　　A 2　　　　27. Service

27. Service of any originating or other notice shall be effected either by personal service of a copy thereof, or by leaving a copy thereof at the house or place of residence of the person intended to be served, or at his office, warehouse, counting-house, shop, factory, or place of business, with the wife, child, father, mother, brother, sister, or any other relative of the person intended to be served, or with any relative of his wife, or with any servant or clerk of the person intended to be served, the person with whom such copy shall be left being of the age of 16 years and upwards, or by registered letter in the cases hereinafter mentioned. The original notice shall be retained by the party effecting the service.

28. When the person intended to be served is the landlord, service upon his land-agent, to whom the tenant's rent has been usually paid, shall be deemed sufficient service on the landlord.

29. Whenever in any notice served on behalf of the landlord, the address in Ireland of such landlord or of his agent is stated, pursuant to the forms hereby settled, service of any future notice on such landlord in the same proceeding may be effected by registered letter directed to such address of the landlord or agent, until a change of such address has been notified to the Court and the opposite party.

30. Whenever in any notice served by or on behalf of the tenant, the Post Office from which such tenant receives his letters is stated pursuant to the forms hereby settled, service of any future notice on such tenant in the same proceeding may be effected by registered letter directed to such tenant at such Post Office.

31. The receipt of the Post Office for a registered letter proved to have been duly directed to the party intended to be served, and proved to have contained a true copy of the notice required to be served, shall be sufficient prima facie proof of due service on the party to whom it is directed. A letter shall be deemed to have been duly directed to the party intended to be served when it has been directed to him at the address stated by him to be his address, in a notice, or, if more than one, the last notice served by him on the party sending the letter. The statement by a tenant in his notice of the Post Office from which he receives his letters shall, for the purpose of this rule, be deemed a statement of his address until he notifies to the Court and to the opposite party a change of address.

32. An originating notice may be signed by landlord or tenant without a solicitor, or it may be signed by or in the name and by the authority of a solicitor for landlord or tenant.

33. Where landlord or tenant served with an originating notice desires then to be represented by a solicitor, the first notice served on behalf of such landlord or tenant after the originating notice shall be signed by or in the name and by the authority of such solicitor.

34. In no case shall the name of a solicitor be appended to a notice without his authority. Any notice served in violation of this rule may be treated by the Court as a nullity.

35. When at any stage a party not previously represented by a solicitor desires to be so, his solicitor shall serve upon the opposite party notice of his appointment, and shall transmit a copy thereof to the Clerk of the Peace or the Land Commission, as the case may be.

36. Any party shall be at liberty at any time to change his solicitor by notice served by the new solicitor on the former solicitor, and also on the opposite party, and the Clerk of the Peace or Land Commission, as the case may be. The Court shall have power, on the application of the former solicitor, to stay the proceedings until his costs are paid, or to make an order directing the client to pay such costs.

37. Every notice signed by a solicitor shall state the address of the office at which notices on him are to be served. In every case in which a party is represented by a solicitor, service upon such solicitor at the address so given shall

shall be the proper mode of serving such party, and notices may either be served by being left at such address, or else transmitted to such address by registered letter.

38. Notices may be served upon the Land Commission or the Clerk of the Peace respectively through the Post, directed to the Secretary of the Land Commission, Merrion-street, Dublin ; or the Clerk of the Peace at his office in the county town. Documents required to be transmitted to the Land Commission or the Clerk of the Peace may be sent and directed in like manner.

39. Any affidavits to be used in the Civil Bill Court under the Act may be sworn before a Commissioner for taking Affidavits in any Superior Court, or before any Clerk of the Peace, or any Justice of the Peace, and shall, before being used, be lodged with the Clerk of the Peace of the county in which such Civil Bill Court shall be held.

40. Any affidavit to be used before the Land Commission may be sworn before a Commissioner for taking Affidavits in any Superior Court, or before any Justice of the Peace, and shall, before being used, be transmitted to the Secretary of the Land Commission, or lodged with the Sub-Commission if sitting.

41. Certified copies of affidavits shall, if obtained from the Clerk of the Peace, be certified by him, and if obtained from the Land Commission shall be certified by the Registrar or Assistant Registrar.

42. In cases before the Land Commission, copies of affidavits made by the parties shall, if transmitted with the originals, be compared and certified by the Registrar or Assistant Registrar free of charge.

43. Certified copies of documents other than affidavits required from the Land Commission shall be certified by an officer of the proper department. Certified copies shall (except under Rule 42) be paid for at the rate of three halfpence per folio of 72 words.

44. All affidavits shall be expressed in the first person of the deponent, and drawn up in paragraphs and numbered.

45. All affidavits, other than those for which forms are given in the schedule, shall state the deponent's occupation, quality, and place of residence, and also in the usual form his age, and also what facts or circumstances deposed to are within deponent's own knowledge, and his means of knowledge, and what facts or circumstances deposed to are known to or believed by him by reason of information derived from other sources than his own knowledge, and what such sources are.

46. Summonses for the attendance of witnesses and production of documents before the Land Commission or any Sub-Commission shall be in Form No. 42, and shall be signed by the Registrar or Assistant Registrar of the Land Commission, or by any member of a Sub-Commission, or by the Clerk of the Peace ; and in all proceedings in the Civil Bill Court under the Act such summonses shall be signed by the Clerk of the Peace.

47. When the same question is substantially raised in two or more cases for hearing before the same Court, or where it shall for any reason seem expedient to the Court, it shall be lawful for the Court by order to direct that such cases shall be heard together, or that the proceedings in any one or more of such cases may be stayed, and the Court shall have the same power of consolidating proceedings as the High Court of Justice has with respect to actions.

48. The Court shall have power, in any proceedings pending before it, to direct any person appearing to have an interest, to be served with notice of the proceedings, and such person shall thereupon have the same rights of appearing, intervening, and being served with notice, as if he had been a person named in the originating notice or proceeding, either as landlord or tenant, and shall, if the Court so order, be bound by the proceedings. A person so directed to be served shall be served with a notice which may be in Form No. 43.

49. Whenever the Civil Bill Court has cognizance of any case under the Act, the case shall be heard at the Land Sessions next after the originating notice, if such notice has been served a month before the first day of the Land Sessions, otherwise at the following Land Sessions.

50. The Clerk of the Peace, by himself or his deputy, or the principal assistant of the Clerk of the Crown and Peace, shall, if required, be bound to attend the sittings of the Land Commission and Sub-Commissions, at the respective times and places at which either the Land Commission or any Sub-Commission shall sit for cases arising within his county, and produce all books, records, and documents relating to the cases to be tried.

51. It shall be the duty of the Clerk of the Peace to enter every originating notice in a book to be called the "Land Law Act Case Book," in consecutive numbers, and also to transmit the duplicate notice received by him to the Secretary of the Land Commission; and every notice served on the Clerk of the Peace subsequently in the same case, shall be likewise noted in the said book under the same number, and the duplicate thereof shall be transmitted to the Secretary of the Land Commission. It shall be the duty of the Clerk of the Peace to transmit to the Secretary of the Land Commission certified copies of all orders made by the Judge of the Civil Bill Court under the Act.

52. The Registrar of the Land Commission shall enter an abstract of every originating notice received by the Secretary from any Clerk of the Peace in a book, to be called the "Land Law Act Case Book," according to counties and in consecutive numbers, and shall enter every subsequent notice and order in the same case, received from the Clerk of the Peace, in such book under the same number.

53. The Registrar of the Land Commission shall enter an abstract of every originating notice served on the Land Commission in books kept according to counties, and shall enter every subsequent notice in the same case in the proper book under the same number. When the case is ready to be heard by any Sub-Commission, the notices served in each such case shall be transmitted to the Sub-Commission, and shall be returned with the order of the Sub-Commission to the Land Commission.

54. The process servers of any county or riding, or the summons servers of any Petty Sessions district, may be employed, within their respective districts, to serve notices under the Act whether originating or otherwise, and each of them so employed shall be entitled to charge 1s. as a fee for the service or services of each notice, whether originating or otherwise, for which fee he shall be bound to serve a copy on the party or parties, and transmit by post one copy to the Land Commission, at their office, in Dublin, or two copies to the Clerk of the Peace, as the case may be, the party employing him paying the postage, if any, and he shall be further bound to endorse on the copy sent to the Land Commission, or one of the copies sent to the Clerk of the Peace, the time and mode of service of the party or parties served, and he shall be further bound to endorse on the original the time and mode of service as well of the parties as of the Clerk of the Peace or Land Commission.

55. It shall be also the duty of process servers and summons servers, when required, to attend in Court and prove the service and posting of notices.

56. Where such attendance is before the Land Commission or any Sub-Commission, the process servers or summons servers may be allowed for their expenses in so attending, such sum to be paid by such party as the Commission or Sub-Commission may direct.

57. Whenever money is to be paid into Court, pursuant to the Act or these rules, such payment shall be made into the branch bank of the Bank of Ireland in the respective counties, or, if no such branch exists in the county, then into such other bank or branch bank, for transmission to the Bank of Ireland, as the Land Commission shall direct.

58. To effect such payments into Court, where the Court having jurisdiction shall be the Civil Bill Court, the person paying shall obtain a docket, signed by the Clerk of the Peace for the time being, which may be in Form No. 44,
authorising

authorising the lodgment of the sum in the bank in the name of the Clerk of the Peace for the time being, to the credit of the matter specified by number and county, and, on making such lodgment, the person making such lodgment shall deliver or transmit by registered letter to the Clerk of the Peace the bank receipt for such lodgment.

59. No money so lodged shall be drawn out without an order of the Judge of the Civil Bill Court, made on consent in writing of the parties, or, upon application of any of the parties, and notice to the others.

60. Where any lodgment shall have been so made, the amount lodged shall be paid out only on a cheque, signed by the Clerk of the Peace for the time being, and countersigned by the Judge of the Civil Bill Court.

61. To effect such payments into Court, where the Court having jurisdiction shall be the Land Commission, the person paying shall obtain a docket, signed by the Secretary of the Land Commission, which may be in Form No. 45, authorizing the lodgment of the sum in the bank in the name of the Irish Land Commission, and no money so lodged shall be drawn out without an order of the Land Commission, made on the consent in writing of the parties, or on application of any of the parties, and notice to the others, nor shall any money so lodged be paid out except on a cheque, signed by a Commissioner, and countersigned by the Secretary of the Commission, or in his absence, by a second Commissioner.

62. Where proceedings have been commenced in the Civil Bill Court, the application to the Land Commission to transfer such proceedings from the Civil Bill Court to the Land Commission, may be made one week, at least, before the first day of the sitting of the Civil Bill Court for civil business at the Sessions at which the case would otherwise have been heard. Notice of such application shall be given to the Clerk of the Peace, and to the opposite party, and also to the Land Commission. It may be in Form No. 46, and there shall be sent therewith to the Land Commission a copy of the originating notice. Cause against the making of such order, specifying grounds by reason of which such transfer would be unjust or unreasonable, may be shown within one fortnight after service of such notice. Cause may be shown by notice in Form No. 47. If no cause be shown, an order of transfer will be made as of course, at the expiration of said period of one fortnight, and a certified copy of such order shall be sent down by the Commission to the Clerk of the Peace. Where cause is shown, the application for transfer shall be heard and determined by the Land Commission, evidence being given by affidavit, unless the Court shall direct it to be given in some other way.

63. The Clerk of the Peace shall within one month after receiving the same, forward to the Land Commission a copy of every award recorded under Section 25 of the "Landlord and Tenant (Ireland) Act, 1870," or Section 40 of the Act.

64. Every order of one member of the Land Commission shall be signed by him, and every order of a Sub-Commission shall be signed by the members of such Sub-Commission, and every order shall be dated and bear date as of the day on which it is signed.

65. Any person aggrieved by any order of one Commissioner, or by any order of a Sub-Commission, may, within one fortnight after the date of such order, serve, on the opposite party and the Land Commission, a notice which may be in Form No. 48, requiring his case to be reheard, pursuant to Section 44 of the Act.

66. Any person aggrieved by the decision of any Civil Bill Court, with respect to the determination of any matter under the Act, or any part of any Act incorporated therewith, or under the Landlord and Tenant (Ireland) Act, 1870, may, within one fortnight from the last day of the ordinary sessions in the town in which such decision shall have been made, give notice of appeal in writing to the opposite party, and shall also, within the same period, lodge two copies of such notice with the Clerk of the Peace, who shall transmit one of such copies to the Land Commission. The time and place of hearing such appeal shall be duly notified.

67. The statement of a case in respect of any question of law proposed to be submitted by way of appeal to Her Majesty's Court of Appeal in Ireland, shall be prepared by the party making such application, and, after having been submitted to the opposite party, who shall be at liberty to make such observations and alterations thereon as he shall think fit, shall be settled by the Land Commission, and shall be filed, and a certified copy thereof transmitted to the Registrar of the Court of Appeal for hearing. It shall be the duty of the party in whose favour the Court of Appeal shall have decided to cause a certified copy of the order of the Court of Appeal to be lodged with the Registrar of the Land Commission with all convenient speed.

68. Consents on the part of the Land Commission shall be signified under their seal, and consents of any corporation shall be signified under the seal of such corporation, and consents by individuals shall be signified in writing under their hands, and, in the case of a marksman, his signature shall be witnessed by some person who shall certify by writing under his hand, that the consent was duly read over to such marksman, and that he fully understood the same.

SALE OF TENANCIES.

69. A tenant intending to sell his tenancy shall give notice to his landlord, which may be in the Form No. 1 annexed to these rules.

70. Within one fortnight from the service of such notice the landlord, if he desire to purchase the tenancy, and if he has disagreed with the tenant in respect of such purchase, may apply to the Court to ascertain the true value of the tenancy, by notice, according to Form No. 2. Such notice shall be served upon the tenant and upon the Clerk of the Peace of the county, or the Land Commission according to the Court chosen.

71. In default of the landlord either agreeing with the tenant to purchase or applying to the Court within the above time, the tenant may at the expiration of the said period of one fortnight, or earlier, with the written consent of the landlord, sell his tenancy pursuant to the Act, and shall thereupon give notice to the landlord of the name of the purchaser, and of the consideration agreed to be given for the tenancy. Such notice may be according to Form No. 3.

72. An application by the landlord to the Court to declare the sale to be void under Section 1, Sub-section 5 of the Act, shall be made to the Court within one fortnight after the sale shall have come to the landlord's knowledge, and such application may be in the Form No. 4.

73. When the landlord intends to refuse to accept the purchaser as tenant on alleged reasonable grounds, he shall, within one fortnight after receiving the notice of the name of the purchaser, serve a notice on the tenant, which may be in the Form No. 5.

74. If the tenant dispute the reasonableness of the landlord's refusal, he shall, within one fortnight after receiving the landlord's Notice No. 5, serve upon the landlord, and also upon the Clerk of the Peace of the county, or the Land Commission, as the case may be, a notice which may be in the Form No. 6, and shall therewith send to the Clerk of the Peace, or the Land Commission, the landlord's Notice No. 5, or a copy thereof.

75. In case the landlord object to the purchaser and assert that his objection is conclusive, by reason of such permanent improvements as are mentioned in Section 1, Sub-section 6, of the Act, having been made and substantially maintained by him or his predecessors in title, and not by the tenant or his predecessors in title, he shall, within one fortnight after having received notice of the name of the purchaser, give notice to the tenant which may be in Form No. 7.

76. If the tenant dispute the fact of such improvements having been made and substantially maintained by the landlord and his predecessors in title, he shall, within one fortnight after having received the Notice No. 7, give notice

notice to his landlord, and to the Clerk of the Peace of the county, or the Land Commission, which notice may be in Form No. 8, and he shall therewith transmit to the Clerk of the Peace, or the Land Commission, the landlord's Notice No. 7, or a copy thereof.

77. Where the landlord, on the application of the tenant, consents that his property in improvements shall be sold along with the tenancy, pursuant to Section 1, Sub-section 8, of the Act, such consent may be in Form No. 9.

78. Where the landlord's property in improvements is so sold accordingly, the landlord and tenant jointly, or either separately, shall, within one fortnight after the sale, give notice to the Clerk of the Peace of the county, or the Land Commission, which may be in Form No. 10. If the application be not made jointly the party applying shall within the same period serve a copy of the notice on the opposite party.

79. A landlord making a claim in respect of arrears of rent or other breaches of the contract or conditions of tenancy, shall give notice to the outgoing tenant and to the purchaser, which may be in Form No. 11. Such notice shall be given within one fortnight after the landlord receives notice of the name of the purchaser, if the landlord does not object to the purchaser; or, in case the landlord does object to the purchaser, then within one fortnight after such objection shall have been adjudicated upon or withdrawn.

80. If the outgoing tenant does not, within one fortnight after receiving Notice No. 11, give notice to the purchaser that he disputes the landlord's claim, or any part thereof, the purchaser shall, on the expiration of such period of one fortnight, pay to the landlord, out of the purchase-money, the amount of such claim.

81. If the outgoing tenant dispute such claims, or any of them, he shall within the said period of one fortnight after receiving Notice No. 11, give notice to the landlord and to the purchaser, which may be in Form No. 12, specifying the amount which he admits and the amount which he disputes, and the purchaser shall thereupon forthwith pay to the landlord the amount admitted, if any, and shall pay the residue into Court in the manner by these rules provided.

82. Where a sale of a tenancy is about to take place under a writ of execution by any execution creditor other than the landlord, such execution creditor shall, at least one fortnight before the day of sale, give notice both to the landlord and to the tenant of his intention to sell, and when the landlord is himself the execution creditor he shall within the same period give like notice to the tenant. Such notice may be in Form No. 13, varied according as the landlord is or is not the person serving the notice.

83. Thereupon it shall be competent for the landlord, within the said period of a fortnight, if he desire to purchase the tenancy, to serve notice of application to the Court to ascertain the true value thereof, which notice may be in Form No. 14, and shall be served on the tenant, the sheriff, the execution creditor, and also on the Clerk of the Peace, or the Land Commission, as the case may be.

84. In case the landlord does not serve the notice prescribed by the preceding rule within the time aforesaid, the sheriff may proceed to sell according to the exigency of the writ lodged with him.

85. Where the landlord is himself the execution creditor, and is desirous to purchase the tenancy, otherwise than at the sheriff's sale, he shall give both to the tenant and to the sheriff notice of application to the Court to ascertain the value of the tenancy within one fortnight after the lodgment of the writ with the sheriff, which notice may be in Form No. 15. The purchase-money so ascertained shall be paid by the landlord to the sheriff to be dealt with by him as if the same were obtained at public sale, provided that if the landlord would have been entitled in that capacity to receive all or portion of the purchase-money if the sale had been made by the sheriff in the ordinary way, he shall be entitled to retain the whole or portion of the value ascertained by the Court, as the

33. B

the case may be; and in case of dispute the amount so to be retained shall be settled by the Court.

86. When the sale takes place by the personal representative of a deceased tenant, he shall give notice in the landlord of the intention to sell, which notice may be in Form No. 16, stating therein that he gives the notice in his capacity of personal representative; and if the landlord desires to purchase he shall, within one fortnight after receipt of such notice, serve notice of application to the Court to purchase the tenancy, and the future proceedings shall be carried out in the same manner as in the case of a tenant himself selling.

87. Where the sale takes place by the assignee in bankruptcy of the tenant, or by a person having carriage of sale of the tenancy under the order of any Court, the assignees, or the person having carriage of the sale, shall give notice to the landlord and tenant of the intended sale, which notice may be in Form No. 17, and thereupon the landlord shall, within one fortnight from receipt of the notice, if he desire to purchase the tenancy, serve notice of application to the Court to ascertain the true value thereof, which notice may be in Form No. 14, and shall be served on the tenant, the person selling, and the Clerk of the Peace, or the Land Commission, as the case may be.

88. In all cases not provided for by the foregoing Rules, it shall be lawful for the Court, on application, to name a person by and on whom, in place of the tenant, notices shall be served respecting the sale of a tenancy.

89. When the landlord does not himself purchase the tenancy, his notice of objection to the purchaser may be in Form No. 5 or No. 7, as the case may be, and shall be served on the personal representative of the tenant, the assignee in bankruptcy of the tenant, the person having carriage of the sale, or execution creditor, as the case may be, and where the tenant is living, the notice shall also be served on him.

90. Notice pursuant to Section 1, Sub-section 16, of the sum claimed to be due to the landlord for arrears of rent, or on account of breaches of the contract or conditions, may be given in Form No. 18 by the landlord to the tenant within one fortnight after receiving notice from the tenant of the intended sale of the tenancy, and if the tenant dispute the amount so claimed, and determine to proceed with the sale, he shall give notice of application to the Court, which may be in Form No. 19; and if no purchaser be found within three months after the service of the landlord's notice, No. 18, to give the same or a greater sum, the landlord may make application to the Court to be adjudged the purchaser of the tenancy at the sum so claimed by him, which application may be in Form No. 20.

91. Notice served on the landlord nominating a person to succeed to the tenancy, pursuant to Section 3 of the Act, may be in Form No. 21, and if the landlord object to accept such person as tenant on such grounds as would have entitled him to object in the case of a sale of the tenancy, he shall give to the personal representative of the deceased tenant a notice, which may be in Form No. 22, or in Form No. 23, as the case may require. If the landlord's grounds of refusal are disputed, the personal representative may serve an originating notice seeking the decision of the Court, which notice may be according to Form No. 6 or No. 8, as the case may be, with the necessary changes.

92. If the landlord require a sale to be made under Section 3, he shall give to the personal representative of the deceased tenant notice, which may be in Form No. 24, and if the personal representative fail to sell the same, pursuant to the statute, the landlord may make application to the Court in Form No. 25, and thereupon the Court may direct the landlord to proceed to sell the tenancy by auction, in such manner and with such conditions as it may think fit, and may direct all proper persons to concur in the assignment to the purchaser, and the purchase-money shall be brought into Court to abide such order as the Court shall think fit to make regarding it.

93. An application by the landlord to the Court for resumption of the holding, or part thereof, pursuant to Section 5, or to Section 8, Sub-section 3, of the Act, may be in Form No. 96.

FAIR RENT.

94. An application to the Court to fix a fair rent may be made by notice in Form No. 27 or No. 28, as the case may be, and, unless where such application is made by the landlord and tenant jointly, a copy shall be served upon the opposite party. An application to fix a fair rent shall not be withdrawn save by leave of the Court, given on consent, or on due notice to the opposite party.

95. A certified copy of the Order, fixing the judicial rent, may be had by the landlord and tenant respectively, on application to the Land Commission and payment of a fee of 1 s.

96. When the landlord intends to submit to the Court that the tenant's application to fix a fair rent should be disallowed on the grounds mentioned in Section 6, Sub-section 4, he may serve notice in Form No. 29.

97. When either landlord or tenant makes application to the Court to fix a specified value of the tenancy on the occasion of any application to fix a judicial rent, he shall, one week at least before the application to fix a judicial rent is heard, serve notice thereof, which may be in Form No. 30, and a certified copy of the Order fixing such specified value may be obtained by the landlord and tenant respectively, on application to the Land Commission on payment of a fee of 1 s.

98. Wherever a specified value for the tenancy has been fixed, and the landlord, having received notice of the tenant's intention to sell, claims to purchase the tenancy, but there is a disagreement between the landlord and the tenant as to the amount to be paid for such tenancy, having regard to the provisions of Section 6, Sub-section 5 of the Act, either party may make application to the Court to ascertain the amount of the purchase-money under the said Sub-section, and the said application may be in Form No. 31, or Form No 32, as the case may be. If the landlord's notice under this rule be first served, the tenant shall be bound to serve his notice within one fortnight after receiving the landlord's notice, and if the tenant's notice be first served, the landlord shall serve his notice within one fortnight after receiving the tenant's notice.

99. Either party may demand from the other before the hearing of such application, and, if necessary, may apply to the Court for particulars of the case intended to be made, either as to increase of value by means of improvements or diminution of value by dilapidation of buildings or deterioration of soil.

100. Where the landlord and tenant agree what is the then fair rent of the holding, pursuant to Section 8, Sub-section 6, or Section 20, Sub-section 2, they shall enter into an agreement and declaration, which may be in Form No. 33, and the tenant's signature thereto shall be witnessed by a clergyman, by a solicitor, by a commissioner for taking affidavits, by a justice of the peace, or by a poor law guardian ; but the witness must not in any case be a person in the employment of the landlord.

101. Where the tenant is a marksman, the witness to his signature must also certify under his hand that the declaration and agreement has been read and explained to the tenant in his presence.

102. The declaration and agreement aforesaid shall, within one month after the date thereof, be lodged with the clerk of the peace of the county, or with the Land Commission, as the case may be, and the clerk of the peace or Land Commission shall file the same at the expiration of three months from the lodgment thereof, if no notice of objection to the filing thereof shall have been in the meantime received : or it may be filed at such other time as the Court shall direct : and on the same being filed the Civil Bill Court or the Land Commission shall give to the landlord and tenant respectively, a certificate in Form No. 34, on payment of a fee of 1 s. for each.

103. Where the declaration and agreement is lodged with the clerk of the peace a copy thereof shall be also lodged with him, which it shall be his duty forthwith to transmit to the Land Commission.

104. The Land Commission may direct periodical notices of the lodgment of all declarations and agreements, whether with the clerk of the peace or with the Land Commission, to be published in such newspapers as it shall think fit.

105. It shall be lawful for either landlord or tenant, or any incumbrancer or other person having an interest, within three months from the lodgment of any such declaration and agreement, to serve notice on the clerk of the peace or the Land Commission, as the case may be, and also on the parties or opposite party of an application that the said declaration and agreement be not filed on the ground of fraud or surprise, or some other sufficient ground stated in such notice, and supported by affidavit, and thereupon the said declaration and agreement shall not be filed without the order of the Court, and either party may apply on notice for such order.

JUDICIAL LEASES AND FIXED TENANCIES.

106. When the landlord and tenant agree to a judicial lease pursuant to Section 10, the landlord shall cause a draft of such lease to be prepared, containing such provisions as may have been agreed on between the parties. Such draft shall be transmitted either to the Clerk of the Peace or to the Secretary of the Land Commission according to the Court selected, together with a notice of application which may be in Form No. 35, containing the particulars therein mentioned. And notice of such application, which may be in Form No. 36, shall be served upon the tenant and also upon the mortgagees of the interests of the landlord and tenant respectively, and on such other incumbrancers, and such trustees, persons in remainder, and other persons as the landlord shall deem expedient, having regard to the state of his title, and the Court may at any time direct such verification of the particulars, and such further inquiries to be made, notices to be served, documents to be furnished, and advertisements to be published, as it shall deem fit.

107. Where the draft lease is approved of by the Court, such approval shall be signified by an endorsement on the draft signed by the County Court Judge or a Commissioner, or by the members of a Sub-Commission, as the case may be, and the lease shall be engrossed in duplicate from such draft, and when executed by the parties shall also be signed by the County Court Judge or sealed with the seal of the Commission, as the case may be.

108. Where the landlord, being a limited owner, and the tenant agree that the tenancy shall become a fixed tenancy, such agreement shall be embodied in writing, which may be in Form No. 37, and attested as to the tenant's signature in manner prescribed by Rule No. 100, and the same shall be transmitted to the Clerk of the Peace or the Land Commission, together with a notice of the particulars specified in Form No. 35, and the further proceedings therein up to and including the execution of a grant constituting the fixed tenancy shall be as in the case of proceedings for Judicial leases, and the grant shall be approved by the Court.

RULES RELATING TO PART IV. OF THE ACT.

109. Any application to the Land Commission under Section 13, Sub-Section 4, of the Act may be made in Form No. 38, and shall be based on affidavit of the tenant setting forth the grounds of such application. Notice of the application shall be served upon the landlord and on the Land Commission at least a week before the hearing of such application, and the landlord and tenant respectively may give evidence of the facts by affidavit or otherwise as they think fit, and if

by

by affidavit, the last of such affidavits shall be filed at least two days before the hearing.

110. Notice of application by a tenant to let portion of a holding for the use of labourers shall state whether the situation has or has not been approved of by the landlord, and shall also state whether the portion is proposed to be let with or without dwelling-houses, and upon what terms as to rent the letting is proposed to be made, and the contents, as accurately as possible, of the portion proposed to be let, and also the number of acres of tillage land in the entire holding; such application may be in Form No. 89, and a copy of such notice shall be served upon the landlord at least one week before the hearing.

111. Notice of application by a landlord to resume the holding pursuant to Section 21 of the Act, may be in Form No. 40, and shall be served on the tenant of the holding, either during the last three months of the lease or other contract of tenancy, or within three months after the termination of such lease or other contract of tenancy.

112. An application by a tenant holding under a lease accepted by him since the 1st August 1870, to have such lease declared void on the grounds mentioned in Section 21 of the Act, may be in Form No. 41, and shall be served upon the landlord, and the application shall not be heard until the lapse of one month from the service of such notice.

113. The evidence given upon any such application, as mentioned in the last preceding rule, shall be given viva voce, unless the Court shall otherwise direct, and where the Court shall be the Land Commission, the application shall be heard before the Commissioners themselves, unless the Land Commission shall by order otherwise direct. The time and place of hearing such applications by the Land Commission shall be duly notified.

114. Application for leave to appeal, under Section 21 of the Act, shall be made within one fortnight after the date of the order sought to be appealed from.

Arrears.

115. Where an application is made under Section 59 of the Act, it may be in Form No. 49, and shall be signed by the landlord or by his agent on his behalf, and by the tenant or tenants who shall concur in such application. It shall, moreover, be verified by the landlord or his agent, as provided for in such form, and it shall be forwarded to the Secretary of the Land Commission.

116. If the tenant or any of the tenants, concurring in an application under Section 59 of the Act, be a tenant or tenants evicted for non-payment of rent since the 1st May 1860, the application shall, in addition to complying with the requirements mentioned in the preceding Rule, contain an undertaking on the part of the landlord to reinstate such evicted tenant or tenants upon the terms in said section set forth.

PART V.

Acquisition of Lands by Tenants.

117. Where an application is made for an advance under Section 24 of the Act, to enable tenants to purchase their holding, then,

(a.) Where such sale is about to be made in consideration of the payment of a principal sum, the application may be made in Form No. 50, which shall be signed by both landlord and tenant, or tenants, and which shall contain the particulars and be verified as therein mentioned.

(b.) When the sale is about to be made, in consideration of the tenant paying a fine and engaging to pay to the landlord a fee-farm rent, the application may be in Form No. 51, and shall be signed by both landlord and tenant, or tenants, and shall contain the particulars and be verified as therein mentioned.

F 3.   B 3   118. Every

118. Every application under the foregoing section, or under Section 26 or 29 of the Act, shall be in duplicate and shall be accompanied by the sheet of the Ordnance 0-inch map. distinguishing thereon the holding or holdings of the tenants in respect of whose holdings application is made, and such; holdings shall be marked with numbers to correspond with the respective numbers of the tenancies in the schedule annexed to the application. The application and accompanying documents shall be forwarded to the Secretary of the Land Commission.

119. When either landlord or tenant desires the sale to be negotiated and completed through the medium of the Land Commission, such application may be in the Form No. 52; and the Land Commission may entertain the application, provided the landlord undertake to pay for the expenses of such negotiation, and completion by per-centage on the purchase-money, according to the scale hereinafter mentioned.

The following shall be the scale until the 31st March 1883 :—

```
                                              £  s.  d.
For the expenses of negotiation, up to and
   including signing of contract  -    -    -  10  - per 100 l.
For subsequent expenses  -    -    -    -  3  -    ,,
   including (if contract be completed) conveyance from landlord
   to tenant, mortgage to Commissioners, Registration and Stamp
   duty.
```

120. On receiving any such application as mentioned above, the Land Commissioners shall take such steps for negotiating and completing the sale, either by sending an officer to communicate orally with the landlord and tenants respectively, or by written communication or otherwise, as may in each case seem advisable.

121. In every case of sale by a landlord to a tenant, the Land Commission may require such statement and verification of title, and such rentals, accounts, and other documents to be furnished and verified as they may think fit.

122. Where a landlord desires to sell his estate, and contemplates the purchase thereof by the Land Commission for the purpose of re-sale to the tenants, he may make application to the Land Commission in Form No. 53, and thereupon the Land Commission may negotiate with the landlord with respect to the price at which he will be willing to sell, and the landlord shall thereupon sign a proposal which may be in Form No. 54, containing an undertaking to pay for the expenses of the sale by him to the Commissioners, according to the following scale :—

```
                                              £  s.  d.
For the expenses up to and including notice
   by the Commission to the landlord of their
   being willing to purchase  -    -    -    -  10  - per 100 l.
Together with the subsequent expenses—that is to say, the actual
   outlay by the Commission in completing the sale.
```

123. Upon such proposal being signed, the Commission shall satisfy themselves that a competent number of the tenants are able and willing to purchase their holdings, and shall obtain from a competent number of the tenants an undertaking to purchase their holdings, which may be in Form No. 55. The Commission will estimate the entire expense of carrying out the sale by them to the tenants, and shall have regard to such estimate in settling the prices at which the respective tenants are to purchase their holdings.

124. In special cases the Commission may, with the assent of the Treasury, reduce the amount to be paid either under Rule 119 or Rule 122, below the scale therein mentioned.

125. The Land Commission, on being satisfied that the purchase is one authorised by the Act, and is desirable, shall notify same to the landlord, and may require the landlord to furnish his abstract of title, which shall be investigated in the usual way on behalf of the Commission.

126. Upon

126. Upon the title being approved of, the tenants shall be called upon to lodge the one-fourth of the purchase-money, or one-half of the fines, as the case may be, and the Commission shall not be deemed bound as having contracted to purchase from the landlord, or to sell to the tenants, until such amounts shall have been lodged, and by such number of tenants as are required by the Act. Thereupon the purchase from the landlord shall be completed, and the Commission shall execute to each tenant who has proposed to pay the whole price of his holding, and who has made the due lodgment, a conveyance of his holding, and shall execute to each tenant who has proposed to purchase in consideration of a fine and a fee-farm rent, and who has made the due lodgment, a fee-farm grant of his holding.

127. When an estate is for sale before the Land Justices of the Chancery Division of the High Court of Justice, and a competent number of the tenants on such estate, or on any lot thereof, are able and willing to purchase their holdings, such tenants, or some or one of them on behalf of the others, may make application to the Commission with a view to the purchase by the Commission of the said estate or lot. Such application may be in Form No. 56, and thereupon the Commission may take such steps as they may deem advisable for the purpose of satisfying themselves of the expediency of the purchase, and of the Commission being indemnified from loss in the same, and, if satisfied, the Commission may purchase such estate or lot.

128. Upon the Commission being declared the purchasers of such estate or lot they shall forthwith call upon the tenant or tenants thereof to lodge to the credit of the Commission the one-fourth part of the purchase-money agreed to be paid by such tenants for their respective holdings, or one-half of the fine, as the case may be, if not already lodged or deposited, and the Commission shall not be deemed to have contracted to sell to the tenants, or any of them, until such amounts shall have been lodged, and by such number of the tenants as are required by the Act,

129. Upon such lodgment being made, the Commission shall execute, to each tenant who has proposed to pay the whole price of his holding, and who has made the due lodgment, a conveyance of his holding, and shall execute to each tenant who has proposed to purchase in consideration of a fine and a fee-farm rent, and who has made the due lodgment a fee-farm grant of his holding.

Emigration.

130. Where any application for the purposes of assisting emigration is made to the Commission, under Section 32 of the Act, full particulars shall be given as to the security proposed for repayment of such advances, and in case of the application being made on behalf of any public body or public company, the constitution of such public body or public company shall be clearly stated, and copies of the Act of Parliament, charter, memorandum of association, and articles of association regulating the same, shall accompany the application.

131. The application shall likewise state the mode in which it is intended to apply the loan, and the provisions for securing the satisfactory shipment, transport, and reception of the emigrants. The Commission may direct such further information to be furnished, and such inquiries to be made as they may deem advisable.

ARBITRATION.

132. The reference of any dispute under "The Land Law (Ireland) Act, 1881," to an Arbitration Court, and the appointment of the arbitrator or the arbitrators and umpire may be in the Form No. 57, and be signed by both parties; and such reference, with the nomination of the arbitrator or arbitrators and umpire, as the case may be, shall be lodged with the Clerk of the Peace or with the Land Commission before the first sitting of the Arbitration Court thereunder.

63.　　　　　　　　B 4　　　　　　　133. The

133. The Clerk of the Peace or the Secretary to the Land Commission shall forthwith, on receipt of such reference and nominations, and on being satisfied by affidavit or statutory declaration as to the signatures thereto, enter the same, the former in the Land Law Case Book, and the latter in a book to be kept by him for the purpose; and thereupon any application or report in the matter of such arbitration may be entertained by the Court, and such order may be made thereon as the Court may think right.

134. Where either party desires the award of a Court of Arbitration to be recorded in the Civil Bill Court, he shall, ten days before the first day of the land session next ensuing the making of such award (if sufficient interval shall exist, and if not, then before the next following session), serve notice on the opposite party of his intention to apply to the Court for such purpose, which application shall be heard, in regular course, according to the practice of the Court, and when he desires it to be recorded by the Land Commission, he may serve notice for that purpose on the opposite party and the Land Commission.

135. On the hearing of such application, the Court may, if it shall think fit, and if such award substantially decides the dispute referred, order the same to be recorded, and the award shall thereupon be duly recorded by the Clerk of the Peace in the Land Law Act Case Book, or by the Registrar of the Land Commission.

136. Reference of a case to an Arbitration Court may be made at any time before the first day of the land session at which such dispute may be entered for hearing, or of the sitting of the Land Commission, or Sub-Commission, for hearing such case, or afterwards with the consent of the Court.

Seal of
the Irish Land
Commission

John O'Hagan.
E. F. Litton.
John E. Vernon.

SCHEDULE OF FORMS.

FORM No. 1.

LAND LAW (IRELAND) ACT, 1881.

* PARTICULARS—(The following particulars must be accurately filled up).

Name of Landlord, and residence of Landlord, if known . . . . . {

Name and Residence of Landlord's Agent, if any . . . . . {

Name and Residence of Tenant . {

Post Office from which Tenant receives his Letters . . . . . {

HOLDING,—

County.	Poor Law Union.	Electoral Division.

† Name by which Lands are known on Ordnance Survey Map,

Area in Statute Measure.			Rent of Holding.			Gross Poor Law Valuation.		
a.	r.	p.	£	s.	d.	£.	s.	d.

‡ This can be ascertained by reference to the Poor Rate Receipts, or from the Clerk of the Union.

Notice of Intention to sell Tenancy.

Take notice, that it is my intention to sell my Tenancy in the above holding.

Dated this   day of   189

Signed,

(To be signed by the Tenant.)

To————

The Landlord of the above holding.

FORM No. 2.

[Heading same as Form No. 1.]

The Proceedings under this Notice are intended to be carried on before the Court.

[State either "Civil Bill Court of the County," or "Land Commission," at choice of party.]

Originating Notice of Application by Landlord to ascertain true Value of Tenancy with a view to Purchase.

Having received notice from you of your intention to sell your tenancy, and having disagreed with you as to the terms of the purchase thereof by me, I, desiring to purchase the same under Clause 1 of the Act, apply to the Court to ascertain the true value thereof.

Dated this   day of   188

Signed,

[To be signed by the Landlord, or by his Agent or Solicitor on his behalf.]

To ————

The Tenant of the above holding.

* These particulars must be prefixed as a heading to each form. In Forms 18, 21, 22, 23, 24, and 25, a slight alteration will be required to meet the case of the tenant being dead.

63.   C

Form No. 3.

[Heading same as Form No. 1.]

Notice by Tenant of the Name of Purchaser (other than Landlord), and of the Consideration agreed to be given.

I have agreed to sell my tenancy in the above holding. The name of the Purchaser is   of   and the consideration agreed to be given by him for the purchase is £

Dated this   day of   188

Signed,

[To be signed by Tenant.]

To———

The Landlord of the above holding.

Form No. 4.

[Heading same as Form No. 1.]

The Proceedings under this Notice are intended to be carried on before the Court

[State either " Civil Bill Court of the County," or " Land Commission," at choice of party.]

Originating Notice by Landlord of Application to declare Sale of Tenancy Void.

I apply to the Court to declare void the sale made or agreed to be made by you of your tenancy in the above holding to   and I make this application because you have failed to

[State either " Give me notice of your intention to sell the tenancy," or, " Give me notice of the name of the purchaser;" or, " Give me notice of the consideration agreed to be given for the tenancy."]

Dated this   day of   188

Signed,

[To be signed by the Landlord, or by his Agent or Solicitor on his behalf.]

To ———

The Tenant of the above holding.

Form No. 5.

[Heading same as Form No. 1.]

Notice of Refusal by Landlord to accept Purchaser as Tenant on reasonable grounds.

I refuse to accept   of   the purchaser named in your notice of the day of   188 , as my Tenant on the following reasonable grounds:—

[State specifically the grounds on which the Purchaser is objected to.]

Dated this   day of   188

Signed,

[To be signed by the Landlord, or by his Agent on his behalf.]

To ———

The Tenant of the above holding.

Form No. 6.

[Heading same as Form No. 1.]

The Proceedings under this Notice are intended to be carried on before the Court.

[State either "Civil Bill Court of the County," or "Land Commission," at choice of party.]

Originating Notice by Tenant of disputing Landlord's grounds of Refusal of Purchaser.

I dispute your grounds of refusal to accept as your tenant   of   , the purchaser of my tenancy in the above holding, and I apply to the Court to declare your grounds of refusal not reasonable.

Dated this   day of   185

Signed.

[To be signed by the Tenant.]

To

The Landlord of the above holding.

Form No. 7.

[Heading same as Form No. 1.]

Notice by Landlord of objection to Purchaser when Improvements have been made and substantially maintained by Landlord or his predecessors.

I assert that the permanent improvements in the above holding, in respect of which, if made by you or your predecessors in title, you would have been entitled to compensation under the provisions of the Landlord and Tenant (Ireland) Act, 1870, as amended by the Land Law (Ireland) Act, 1881, have been made and substantially maintained by me or my predecessors in title, and not by you or your predecessors in title.

And I refuse to accept   of   the purchaser named in your notice of the day of   188 , as my tenant.

Dated this   day of   188

Signed,

[To be signed by the Landlord, or by his Agent on his behalf.]

To

The Tenant of the above holding.

Form No. 8.

[Heading same as Form No. 1.]

The Proceedings under this Notice are intended to be carried on before the Court.

[State either "Civil Bill Court of the County," or "Land Commission," at choice of Party.]

Originating Notice by Tenant that he disputes the fact of improvements having been made and substantially maintained by Landlord or his predecessors.

I dispute your assertion that the improvements mentioned in your Notice of the day of   188 have been made and substantially maintained by you or your predecessors in title, and I consequently dispute the validity of your objection to   of   as the purchaser of my tenancy, and I apply to the Court for its decision.

Dated this   day of   188

Signed,

[To be signed by the Tenant.]

To

The Landlord of the above holding.

Form No. 9.

[Heading same as Form No. 1.]

Notice of consent by Landlord that Improvements made or paid for by him or
his predecessors shall be Sold along with the Tenancy.

"Made or paid for."
"He" or "any pre-
decessors in title."

I consent that the permanent improvements on the above holding which have been
by   shall be sold along with your tenancy in the above holding.

["Solely" or "jointly with you," or "jointly with your predecessors in title."]

Dated this   day of   188

Signed,

[To be signed by the Landlord, or his Agent in his behalf.]

To———

Form No. 10.

[Heading same as Form No. 1.]

County   , No.

The Proceedings under this Notice are intended to be carried on before the
Court.

[State either "Civil Bill Court of the County of   ," or " Land Commission."]

Originating Notice of Application to have Purchase Money of Tenancy and Landlord's Improvements apportioned.

"I" or "we."

The tenancy in, and the Landlord's improvements upon, the above holding having been
sold together, and having produced the sum of £   apply to the Court to
apportion the said sum of £   , as between the respective values of the said tenancy
and the said improvements.

Dated this   day of   188

Signed,

[To be signed by the Landlord and Tenant if application be by both ; by the one making the application
if made by one only.]

To———

The Landlord of the above holding, or the Tenant of the above holding if made by own only ; if made
by both, to be omitted.

Form No. 11.

[Heading same as Form No. 1.]

Notice of claim by Landlord against outgoing Tenant for Arrears of Rent, or
other breaches of the Contract or Conditions of Tenancy.

Take notice, that I claim the sum of £   , of which the following are the particulars :

[State here particulars in respect of which the sum is claimed, as for instance—Arrears of Rent, £
    owing gales ; Breach of a contract to repair, £   ; Total, £.]

Dated this   day of   188

Signed,

[To be signed by the Landlord, or his Agent in that behalf.]

To———

The outgoing Tenant or the Purchaser.

Form No. 12.

[Heading same as Form No. 1.]

Notice by outgoing Tenant admitting or denying that the sums claimed by Landlord are due.

]

["Admit that the sum of £   claimed by the tender of the   day of   18   [" or, "I deny that the sum of £   claimed by the notice of the   day of   18   , or any sum in respect of the matter noted in the said notice [" or, "I adopt that the sum of £   , in respect of (as mentioned in the notice of the   day of   18   )] is due by me; but I deny that any further sum in respect of the matter mentioned in the said notice."]

is due by me,

Dated this   day of   18   .

Signed,

[To be signed by the Tenant.]

To ———— -

The Landlord of the above holding and the Purchaser.

Form No. 13.*

[Heading same as Form No. 1.]

Notice of intention to Sell Holding by Execution Creditor.

Take notice that it is my intention, as an Execution Creditor of the above Tenant, under a judgment for £   dated   , to sell the tenancy in the above holding by Sheriff's sale on the   day of   next.

Dated this   day of   18   .

Signed,

[To be signed by Execution Creditor, or his Solicitor on his behalf. If Landlord be the Execution Creditor that fact should be mentioned.]

To ———— .

The Landlord.

And to ———— .

The Tenant.

Form No. 14.

[Heading same as Form No. 1.]

County   No.

The Proceedings under this Notice are intended to be carried on before the Court.

[State either "Civil Bill Court of the County," or "Land Commission," at choice of party.]

Originating Notice by Landlord of Application to ascertain true value of Tenancy, when Sale is made under a Judgment, or other process of law, against the Tenant, or for the payment of the Debts of a Deceased Tenant.

Having received notice from you as   of the above Tenant of your intention to sell the tenancy, I elect to purchase the same under clause 1 of the Act, and I apply to the Court to ascertain the true value thereof.

Dated this   day of   18   .

Signed,

[To be signed by the Landlord.]

To ———— -

The person serving notice of intention to sell, and, if sale under execution, to the Sheriff of the county and to the Tenant.

* Execution Creditor," "Personal Representative," "Assignee in Bankruptcy," or otherwise, as the case may be.

* Note.—This notice must be served both on Landlord and Tenant, or Tenant alone, if Landlord himself be the Execution Creditor.

Form No. 15.

[Heading same as Form No. 1.]

Conty   No.

The Proceedings under this Notice are intended to be carried on before

(State either "Civil Bill Court of the County," or "Land Commission," at choice of party.)

Originating Notice of Intention to Purchase by Landlord, being also Execution Creditor, and of application to Court to fix Value.

Take notice that I, the above-named Landlord, being also an Execution Creditor of the above-named Tenant, under a writ of   for £   :   :   . elect to purchase the tenancy in the above holding, under clause 1 of the Act, and I apply to the Court to ascertain the true value thereof.

Dated this   day of   186 .

Signed.

[To be signed by the Landlord, or his Agent in that behalf.]

To __ __

The Sheriff of the County of ———

And to ————— .

The Tenant.

Form No. 16.

[Heading as in Form No. 1, with the variation, that in addition to the name and residence of the late Tenant, the name and residence of the Personal Representative, as well as the post office from which the latter receives his letters, should be stated.]

Notice of intention to Sell Tenancy, if given by Personal Representative.

Take notice that it is   intention as   of the said Tenant to sell the tenancy in the above holding.

Dated this   day of   186

Signed,

[To be signed by the Personal Representative.]

To ———— .

The Landlord of the holding.

Form No. 17.

[Heading same as Form No. 1.]

Notice of intention to Sell Holding, if given by Assignees in Bankruptcy or person having carriage of Sale under the Order of any Court.

Take notice that it is   intention as

[" Assignee in Bankruptcy of the above Tenant," or " Having carriage of the sale of the tenancy, under an Order of the Court, dated — day of — 186 "]

to sell the tenancy in the above holding.

Dated this   day of   186

Signed,

[To be signed by the person or persons giving the notice.]

To ————

The Landlord.

To ————

The Tenant.

Form No. 18.

[Heading same as Form No. 1.]

Notice by Landlord of intention to purchase Tenancy as a means of securing the sum due to him for arrears of rent and breaches of contract.

Take notice that I claim that the sum of £   is due to me by you, of which the following are the particulars :—

[State particulars briefly here, as for Instance—Arrears of Rent, specifying gales, £   ; Breach of contract to repair, £   ; Total, £   ]

and that I am not desirous of purchasing your tenancy in the above holding otherwise than as a means of securing the payment of the said sum of £   , but that I claim to be declared the purchaser of the said tenancy at that sum if you determine to proceed with the sale, and if no purchaser can be found within three months after the service of this Notice who will give the said sum of £

Dated this   day of   189

Signed,

[To be signed by the Landlord, or his Agent in that behalf.]

To ————
The Tenant of the above holding.

Form No. 19.

[Heading same as Form No. 1.]

County   , No.

The proceedings under this Notice are intended to be carried on before the Court.

[State whether "Civil Bill Court for the County," or "Land Commission," at choice of party.]

Originating Notice by Tenant disputing sums claimed to be due by Landlord.

I dispute that the sum of £   claimed by your Notice of the   day of   186   is due by me to you; and I apply to the Court to have it claimed by Land determined whether any, and, if any, what sum is due by me to you in respect of the several matters mentioned in your said Notice.

Dated the   day of   186

Signed,

[To be signed by the Tenant.]

To
The Landlord of the above holding.

Form No. 20.

[Heading same as Form No. 1.]

County   , No.

The Proceedings under this Notice are intended to be carried on before the Court.

[State either "Civil Bill Court of the County," or "Land Commission," at choice of party.]

Originating Notice by Landlord of Application to Court to be adjudged the purchaser of a holding at the sum claimed for arrears of rent and Breach of contract.

I apply to the Court to be adjudged the purchaser of your holding at the sum of £   stated as due by you to me in my notice of the   of

Signed,

Dated the   day of   189

[State date of Notice of intention to purchase as means of securing arrears of rent, and breach of contract.]

To ————
The Tenant of the above holding.

Form No. 21.
[Heading as in Form No. 16.]

Notice by Personal Representative of Tenant nominating Person to succeed to Tenancy.

[I (name) or we, the Executors named in the will, dated   day of   188 , or I, the Administrator of the personal estate.]

of the above-named Tenant, hereby nominate

of

[Name and Address of person nominated.]

being a

[Legatee named in the said will, or a person entitled to a share of the personal estate of the said Tenant under the Statute of Distributions.]

to succeed to the Tenancy of the above-named Tenant in the above holding.

Dated this   day of   188

Signed,

[To be signed by the Executor or Executors, Administrator or Administrators.]

To— ——

The Landlord of the above holding.

Form No. 22.
[Heading as in Form No. 16.]

Notice of Refusal by Landlord to accept Legatee or next of kin as Tenant on reasonable grounds.

I refuse to accept   of   the person named in your

[Insert terms of Legatee or next of kin.]

Notice of the   day of   188 , on the following reasonable grounds:—

[State specifically the grounds on which the Legatee or next of kin is objected to.]

Dated this   day of   188

Signed,

[To be signed by the Landlord, or his Agent on his behalf.]

To———

The Executor or Executors, or the Administrator or Administrators of the Tenant.

Form No. 23.
[Heading as in Form No. 16.]

Notice by Landlord of Refusal to accept Legatee or next of kin as Tenant where Improvements have been made and substantially maintained by the Landlord or his predecessors.

I assert that the improvements on the above holding, in respect of which, if made by the Tenant or his predecessors in title, he would have been entitled to compensation under the Landlord and Tenant (Ireland) Act, 1870, as amended by the Land Law (Ireland) Act, 1881, have been made and substantially maintained by me and my predecessors in title, and not by the above-named Tenant or his predecessors in title; and I refuse to accept   of   the person named in your notice of the   day of   188 , as my Tenant.

Dated this   day of   188

Signed,

[To be signed by the Landlord, or by his Agent on his behalf.]

To— — ——

The personal Representative of the Tenant.

FORM No. 24.

[Heading as in Form No. 16.]

Notice by Landlord requiring personal Representative to Sell.

Take notice that as you, being the personal Representative of the above-named Tenant, have not nominated

[Insert " One of the Legatees under his will," or " One of the persons entitled in distribution to his personal estate."]

to succeed to his tenancy in the above holding, I hereby require you to sell the said tenancy.

Dated this   day of   188

Signed.

[To be signed by the Landlord or his Agent on his behalf.]

To ————

The personal Representative of the deceased Tenant

———————————

FORM No. 25.

[Heading as in Form 16.]

County   , No.

The proceedings under this Notice are intended to be carried on before the Court.

[State either " Civil Bill Court of the County," or " Land Commission," at choice of Party.]

Originating Notice of Application to Court by Landlord to Sell Tenancy by reason of default of personal Representative to nominate successor or to sell.

As you, being the personal Representative of the above-named Tenant, have not nominated one of the

[" Legatees under his will," or " Person entitled in distribution to his personal estate."]

to succeed to his tenancy in the above holding, and have failed to sell the said tenancy, although required by me, by notice dated the   day of   188   , to sell the same, I apply to the Court to direct a sale of the said tenancy.

Dated this   day of   188

Signed.

[To be signed by the Landlord, or his Agent on his behalf.]

To ————

The personal Representative of the deceased Tenant.

———————————

FORM No. 26.

[Heading same as Form No. 1.]

The proceedings under this Notice are intended to be carried on before the Court.

[Either " Civil Bill Court of the County of   " or the " Land Commission " at choice.]

Originating Notice by Landlord applying to Court for resumption of whole or part of holding.

I apply to the Court for an order authorising the resumption of the part of the above holding, containing

[If entire holding is sought to be resumed, strike out the words, " the part of," and the subsequent description.]

or thereabouts, and described in the Map or tracing accompanying this Notice, for a reasonable and sufficient purpose, having relation to the good of the

[Holding or estate.]

namely—

[State specifically the purpose.]

Dated this   day of   188

Signed.

[To be signed by the Landlord or Agent in his behalf.]

To ————

The Tenant of the above holding.

———————————

69.   D

FORM No. 1T.

[Heading same as Form No. 1.]

County   , No.

The proceedings under this Notice are intended to be carried on before the Court.

[State either "Civil Bill Court of the County," or "Land Commission," at choice of party.]

Originating Notice of application by Tenant, or Landlord and Tenant jointly, to Court to fix Fair Rent.

the

[Tenant, or Landlord and Tenant, as the case may be.]

apply to the Court for an Order fixing the Fair Rent to be hereafter paid for the above holding.

Dated this   day of   188 .

Signed,

[To be signed by the party or parties making the application.]

To ———

The Landlord if application be not made jointly.

———

FORM No. 2T.

[Heading same as Form No. 1.]

County   , No.

The Proceedings under this Notice are intended to be carried on before the Court.

[State either "Civil Bill Court of the County," or "Land Commission," at choice of Party.]

Originating Notice of application to Court by Landlord to fix Fair Rent.

the Landlord of the above holding, having demanded

[Landlord.]

that the Rent of the above holding should be increased to £   a year, which the Tenant has declined to accept [or having failed to come to an agreement with the Tenant as to the Rent, viz.,   ], apply to the Court for an Order fixing

[Stating specific nature of disagreement.]

the fair rent to be hereafter paid for the above holding.

Dated this   day of   188

Signed,

[To be signed by the party or parties making the application.]

To ———

The Tenant.

FORM No. 29.

[Heading same as Form No. 1.]

Notice by Landlord to resist application to fix Fair Rent.

I submit that you are not entitled to have the rent to be hereafter paid for the above holding fixed by the Court, for I say that the permanent improvements upon the above holding, in respect of which, if made by you or your predecessors in title, you would have been entitled to compensation under the provisions of the Landlord and Tenant (Ireland) Act, 1870, as amended by the Land Law (Ireland) Act, 1881, have been made by me or my predecessors in title, and have been substantially maintained by me and my predecessors in title, and not made or acquired by you or your predecessors in title.

Dated this   day   18

Signed,

[To be signed by the Landlord or his Agent on his behalf.]

To _____

[The Tenant of the above holding.

FORM No. 30.

[Heading same as Form No. 1.]

Notice by Landlord or Tenant to fix specified value of his Tenancy.

When the application mentioned in   Notice of the   day of   My or your.
18   comes on to be heard, I shall apply that the value of   tenancy in the   My or your.
above holding may be declared and specified.

Dated this   day of   18

Signed,

[To be signed by party giving notice, or if party be Landlord, by his Agent.]

To _____

The other Party.

FORM No. 31.

[Heading same as Form No. 1.]

County   No.

The proceedings under this notice are intended to be carried on before the [State either Civil Bill Court of County, or Land Commission, at choice of party.]

To be omitted if Tenant serve his notice first.

Originating Notice by Landlord of application to Court to ascertain amount by which specified value of Tenancy should be increased or diminished.

Having received notice from the Tenant of his intention to sell his tenancy, and being desirous to buy same, but having disagreed with the Tenant as to the price to be paid by me therefor, I apply to the Court to ascertain the amount by which the purchase-money should be increased above or diminished below the value of £   , specified in the order of the   day of   18

Dated this   day of   18

Signed,

[To be signed by the Landlord, or the Agent on his behalf.]

To _____

The Tenant of the holding.

Form No. 32.

[Heading same as Form No. 1.]

County   , No.

The proceedings under this section intended to be carried on before the Court.

[State either Civil Bill Court of County, or Land Commission, at choice of party.]

Originating Notice by Tenant of application to Court to ascertain amount by which specified value of Tenancy should be increased or diminished.

Having given notice to the Landlord of my intention to sell my tenancy, and having disagreed with the Landlord as to the price to be paid to me therefor, I apply to the Court to ascertain the amount by which the purchase-money should be increased above or diminished below the value of £.   , specified in the order of the   day of   188

Dated this   day of   188 .

Signed,

[To be signed by the Tenant.]

To ....

The Landlord of the holding.

Form No. 33.

[Heading same as Form No. 1.]

To the   Court.

Originating Agreement and Declaration fixing Fair Rent of Holding.

We hereby agree and declare that £.   yearly is now the fair rent of the above holding; and we apply to the   Court to file this agreement, to the intent that the said Rent of £.   may be the Judicial Rent of the holding.

[State either "Civil Bill Court of the County," or "Land Commission," at choice of party.]

Dated this   day of   188

Signed,

(1.)

[Signature of Landlord, or of Agent in his behalf.]

(2.)

[Signature of the Tenant. The Tenant's signature must be witnessed by a Clergyman or a Justice of the Peace, or a Poor Law Guardian, but each witness must not be in the employment of the Landlord.]

Signed by   in my presence by

(3.) And I certify that the above agreement and declaration has been read and explained to the Tenant in my presence.

[To be added if Tenant is a markeman, but not otherwise.]

Form No. 34.

[Heading same as Form No. 1.]

Certificate of filing of Agreement and Declaration fixing Fair Rent.

This is to certify that on the   day of   186 , an Agreement
and Declaration in writing, under the hands of the Landlord and Tenant, dated the
          day of   186 , whereby it was agreed and declared that
£   was the fair rent of the above holding, was filed in Court pursuant to the
provisions of Sec. 8, Sub-sec. 8, of the Land Law (Ireland) Act, 1881.

[Signature of Clerk of the Peace or Seal of the Land Commission, as the case may be.]

Form No. 35.

Heading same as Form No. 1.

County   No.

The proceedings under this Notice are intended to be carried on before the
Court.

[State either Civil Bill Court of County of   or Land Commission.]

Originating Notice by Landlord of Application to Court to sanction Judicial Lease.

I apply to the Court to sanction the Lease, a draft of which is herewith transmitted.
I am   owner of the lands comprising the said holding.

[Absolute or limited.]

My interest is

[State interest of limited owner, viz., as Tenant for life or otherwise. To be omitted if Landlord is absolute owner.]

The other persons interested in the said lands are

[Give names and descriptions of other persons interested, viz., persons entitled in remainder, &c., and names of Trustees, if any, in Settlement. To be omitted if Landlord is absolute owner.]

The said lands are subject to the incumbrances mentioned in the schedule hereto.

[To be omitted if the Landlord's interest is unincumbered.]

The persons interested in the said incumbrances are

[To be omitted if the Landlord's interest is unincumbered.]

No person interested in the said lands (*or to my knowledge in the said incumbrances)
is an infant, idiot, lunatic, or married woman, except

[To be omitted if Landlord is absolute owner.   *To be omitted if Landlord's interest is unincumbered.]

The Tenant's interest is

[State either that the Tenant's interest is unincumbered, or if incumbered, state briefly the incumbrance, and in whose vested.]

Dated this   day of   189

Signed,

[To be signed by Landlord, or Agent on his behalf.]

To _____

Clerk of Peace of County, or Secretary of Land Commission.

Form No. 34.

[Heading same as Form No. 1.]

Notice by Landlord to person Interested of Application having been made to sanction Judicial Lease.

Take Notice, that I have applied to the   to sanction a lease

["Civil Bill Court of the County of ," or " Land Commission."]

by me to the above Tenant of the above holding at the rent above stated, for the term of   years, from the   day of   18   and this notice is served on you in order that you, if so advised, may appear upon the hearing of such application.

Dated this   day of   18

Signed,

[To be signed by the Landlord, or his Agent on his behalf.]

To _____

And to the Mortgagee of the Landlord and Tenant respectively, and each other Incumbrancers, and such Trustees, Persons in remainder, or persons as the Landlord shall deem it expedient to serve.

Form No. 37.

[Heading same as Form No. 1.]

Agreement by Landlord and Tenant to create fixed Tenancy.

We agree that the tenancy now existing in the above holding shall become a fixed tenancy upon the following conditions—

The Tenant shall pay the annual fee-farm rent of £   to be subject to revaluation by the Court every   years.

[To be omitted if rent be not intended to be subject to revaluation.]
[As may be agreed on, but not to be less than 15.]

Dated this   day of   18

Signed,

[To be signed by the Landlord, or his Agent on his behalf, and the Tenant. Tenant's signature must be witnessed by a Clergyman, a Solicitor, a Commissioner for taking Affidavits, a Justice of the Peace, or a Poor Law Guardian, but witness must not be in the employment of the Landlord.]

To _____

The Clerk of the Peace for the County or the Land Commission.

Form No. 38.

[Heading same as Form No. 1.]

County   , No.

Originating Notice by Tenant of application to Land Commission to restrain Proceedings on Notice to Quit during the continuance of Statutory Term.

I apply to the Land Commission for an Order restraining you from taking further proceedings to enforce the Notice to Quit, dated the   day of   18 which you have served upon me.

And I undertake to abide such Order as to the payment by me to you of damages for the breach of Statutory Conditions in respect of which you have served the said Notice to Quit and as to Costs as the Land Commission may think fit to make, which application will be based on my affidavit, sworn the   day of   18   a copy of which is herewith sent.

Dated this   day of   18

Signed,

[To be signed by the Tenant.]

To _____

FORM No. 39.

[Heading same as Form No. 1.]

County , No.

The proceedings under this Notice are intended to be carried on before the Court.

[State either "Civil Bill Court of County," or "Land Commission," at choice of party.]

Originating Notice by Tenant of application to Court to authorise letting of Land for the use of Labourers.

The above holding contains statute acres of tillage land.
I apply for the sanction of the Court to my letting acres, roods, perches, of the above holding for the use of Labourers bond fide employed, and required for the cultivation of the holding.

[State whether with or without dwelling-houses.]

The situation of the part of my holding which I propose so to let been approved by the Landlord.

[has or has not.]

In the Schedule endorsed hereon I have set out the quantity of land in each letting, and the rent I propose to charge for each.

Dated this day of 188

Signed,

[To be signed by the Tenant.]

To ____
The Landlord of the holding

FORM No. 40.

[Heading same as Form No. 1.]

County , No.

The proceedings under this Notice are intended to be carried on before the Court.

[State either "Civil Bill Court of County," or "Land Commission," at choice of party.]

Originating Notice by Landlord of application to resume Holding on expiration of Lease existing at the date of the passing of the Land Law (Ireland) Act, 1881.

I apply to the Court for authority to resume the above holding for the purpose of

[Occupying the same as a residence for myself, or occupying the same as a home farm in connexion with any residence, or providing a residence for a member of my family.]

Dated this day of 188

Signed,

[To be signed by the Landlord, or his Agent on his behalf.]

To ____
The Tenant of the Holding.

Form No. 41.

[Heading same as Form No. 1.]

County   , No.

The proceedings under this Notice are intended to be carried on before the
Court.

[State either "Civil Bill Court of County," or "Land Commission," at choice of party.]

Originating Notice by Tenant of application to have Lease accepted since
passing of Landlord and Tenant (Ireland) Act, 1870, declared void.

I apply to the Court for an Order declaring the Lease of the above holding, dated
the   day of   188   , which was accepted by me since the passing
of the Landlord and Tenant (Ireland) Act, 1870, to be void upon the grounds that it
contains terms which were, at the time of such acceptance, unreasonable or unfair to the
tenant, namely—

[State specifically what terms are complained of.]

and that the acceptance thereof was obtained by

[State whether threat of eviction or undue influence, or both.]

Dated this   day of   188

Signed,

[To be signed by the Tenant.

To_____ .

    The Landlord of the holding.

LAND LAW (IRELAND) ACT, 1881.

Form No. 42.

Summons for Witnesses.

[State name of Landlord.]   Landlord

[State name of Tenant.]   Tenant.

Court

[State Civil Bill Court, or Land Commission.]

The undersigned person is hereby required, pursuant to the Statute in that behalf,
personally to appear and give evidence in this case on behalf of

[State the person on whose behalf attendance is required.]

before   at the sittings (or Court

[The Civil Bill Court, or Land Commission.]

House) in the town of   in the County of   on the
day of   at the Sitting of the Court, and so from day to
day until the matter is disposed of, and then and there to produce the documents set forth
in the Schedule annexed hereto, and herein to fail not under the penalty of £.10.

Dated this   day of   18

Signed,

[If the case be before the Civil Bill Court, this Summons must be signed by the Clerk of the Peace. If
the case be before the Land Commission it must be signed by the Registrar, an Assistant Registrar, of the
Land Commission, or by a member of a Sub-Commission, or by the Clerk of the Peace.]

To_____

SCHEDULE.

Date of Document.	Nature of Document.

Form No. 43.

[Heading same as Form No. 1.]
County , No.

Notice to a Party appearing to have an Interest.

A case being pending before the   Court for the purpose
[Scale either "Civil Bill Court of the County," or "Land Commission," at choice of party.]

of

[State purpose, such as fixing a fair rent, or whatever the purpose may be.]

and it appearing that you have, or claim to have, an Interest, take Notice that upon service hereof on you, you shall have the same rights of appearing in Court, of interrvning, and being served with Notice in the case, and you may be heard in the same manner as if you had been a person named in the originating notice herein.

To

Form No. 44.

[Heading same as Form No. 1.]
County , No.

CIVIL BILL COURT—RECEIVABLE ORDER.

No.   County

Notice to Bank to receive Lodgment.

Receive a lodgment of £.   by   which place in any sums to
credit of the above matter and number.

Dated this   day of   18

Signed,

[To be signed by the Clerk of the Peace, or Crown and Peace]

_____ Clerk of the

County of_____

To the Cashiers of the Bank of Ireland.

Form No. 45.

[Heading same as Form No. 1.]
County , No.

Notice to Bank to receive Lodgment.

THE IRISH LAND COMMISSION.

Title of Account,

Receivable Order, No.   County

Name of Payer,

Address,

On or before   18 , please to receive £.   which place to
the credit of the Cash Account of the Irish Land Commission.

Date   18

_____ Secretary of the Irish Land Commission.

To the Cashiers of the Bank of Ireland.

53.   E

FORM No. 46.

[Heading same as Form No. 1.]

County , No.

Notice to transfer Proceedings from Civil Bill Court to Land Commission.

I apply to the Land Commission to transfer the proceedings in this case from the Civil Bill Court of the County of to the Land Commission.

Dated this day of 18

Signed,

[To be signed by party making application for Transfer.]

To_____

The party originating the proceedings, the Clerk of the Peace for the County, and the Secretary of the Land Commission. A copy of the Originating Notice must be served with this notice on the Secretary of the Land Commission.

FORM No. 47.

[Heading same as Form No. 1.]

County , No.

Notice to show cause against application to transfer proceedings from Civil Bill Court to Land Commission.

I show cause against the proceedings upon my Originating Notice of the day of 18 , being transferred from the Civil Bill Court of the County of to the Land Commission, for I say that

[State specifically grounds on which it would be unjust or unreasonable that proceedings should be transferred.]

Dated this day of 18

Signed,

[To be signed by party showing cause.]

To _____

The party applying to have proceedings transferred.

FORM No. 48.

[Heading same as Form No. 1.]

County , No.

Notice requiring Case to be reheard before all three Commissioners.

[State by whom Order made, viz., by Civil Bill Court, Sub-Commission, or Single Commissioner.]

I am aggrieved by the Order of made at on the day of 188 , whereby it has

[State substance of Order.]

and I require my case to be reheard before the three Land Commissioners sitting together.

Dated this day of 18

Signed,

FORM No. 49.

N.B.—All applications must be made in duplicate.

LAND LAW (IRELAND) ACT, 1881.

To the Irish Land Commission.

I, of , the Landlord of the holdings set forth in the Schedule hereto, each of which said holdings is valued, under the Acts relating to the valuation of rateable property in Ireland, at a sum not exceeding 30 l. a year, do hereby apply to the Irish Land Commission for an advance of the sum of £. pursuant to Section 49 of the Act.

The several Tenants named in said Schedule have paid me sums which I am willing to accept in full discharge of the rents of their respective holdings, payable in respect of the year ending 1881.

[The gale day next before the 22nd August 1881.]

The arrears set out in column H of said Schedule, opposite the names of the several tenants, and which said arrears accrued due on or prior to the day of 1880, are justly and

[The gale day next before the 22nd August 1880.]

truly due by them respectively to *

[* State whether all the arrears are due to Landlord alone, or partly to him and partly to his predecessors, or their representatives, and, if to his predecessors, state how much is due to Landlord and how much to his predecessors.]

I hereby undertake to repay to the Irish Land Commission the said sum of £. or such other sum as they shall advance to me in pursuance of this application, by thirty half-yearly payments, calculated at the rate of £4, 10 s. per centum per annum on the amount advanced.

[The payments will be made on 1st January and 1st July, or on 1st April and 1st October, according to the date at which the advance is made.]

* I also undertake to reinstate in their holdings, on the terms mentioned in the said Section 59, the tenants in said Schedule who have been evicted for non-payment of rent since 1st May 1880, and after whose names in said Schedule the word "Evicted" is placed.

[* This paragraph may be struck out if there be no such tenants named in the Schedule.]

Dated this day of 185

(Signature),

[To be signed by the Landlord or by his Agent.]

I, of (the duly appointed Land Agent of)

[This affidavit may be made by the Landlord or by his Agent. If made by the Landlord himself strike out the words in Italics.]

the above-named Landlord, make oath and say as follows:—I have read the above application, and likewise the Schedule hereto annexed, and I say that the statements contained in said Application and Schedule respectively are true in every particular.

Sworn before me this day of 188

[This affidavit may be sworn before a Justice of the Peace or a Commissioner for taking affidavits.]

We, the several Tenants whose names and holdings are set forth in the Schedule annexed hereto, do hereby join in the above application, and we have signified our assent to it by signing our names opposite to our respective holdings in the column of said Schedule marked H, and we agree to pay to our Landlord the sums set opposite to our names respectively in column J of said Schedule for fifteen years as an addition to whatever rent may be payable by us.

83. E 2 The

The Holdings are situate in the County of _____ Barony of _____ Poor
Law Union of _____ Electoral Division of _____

Left hand.

Margin for Binding to be Left Blank.	A No.	B Name by which Townland is known on Ordnance Map.	C Name of Estate (where Estated) or "Unestated" after the Name).	D Post Office from which Tenant receives his Letters.	E Area of Holding in Statute Measure.	F Gross Poor Law Valuation of Holding.
					A. R. P.	£ s. d.

Right hand.

G Yearly Rent of Holding.	H Amount of Arrears Due up to the 1890.	I Amount of Advance now applied for.	J Annual Amount to be added to Tenants' Rent for 15 Years.	K Signature of Tenant.	L Name, Address, and Description of Person Witnessing Signature of Tenant.	M Observations.
£ s. d.	£ s. d.	£ s. d.	£ s. d.			

ENDORSEMENT.

Section 49 of Irish Land Act, 1881, under which the Advance within applied for is authorised.

CLAUSE LIX.—Where it appears to the Court, on the joint application of the landlord and tenant of any holding valued under the Acts relating to the valuation of rateable property in Ireland, at a sum not exceeding thirty pounds a year—

That the tenant has paid the whole (or such sum as the landlord may be willing to accept as the equivalent of the whole) of the rent payable in respect of the year of the tenancy expiring on the gale day next before the passing of this Act, and that antecedent arrears are due, the Land Commission may make, in respect of such antecedent arrears, an advance of a sum not exceeding one year's rent of the holding, and not exceeding half the antecedent arrears; and thereupon the Court shall by order declare the holding to be charged with the repayment of the advance to the Land Commission, by a rentcharge payable half-yearly during the fifteen years from the date specified in the order, and calculated at the rate of eight pounds ten shillings a year for every hundred pounds of the advance. Whenever in the case of any tenant evicted for non-payment of rent since the first day of May, one thousand eight hundred and eighty, the landlord agrees to reinstate such tenant on the terms in this section set forth, this section shall apply as if such tenant had not been so evicted from his holding.

The charge declared by the order as aforesaid shall have priority over all charges affecting the holding, except quit-rent and Crown-rent, and sums payable to the Commissioners

sioners of Public Works or the Commissioners of Church Temporalities in Ireland, and the landlord for the time being of the holding shall pay to the Land Commission the sum for the time being due on account of such rentcharge.

Every half-yearly amount of such rentcharge shall be deemed to be an addition to the half-year's rent of the holding (whether a judicial rent or otherwise) due from the tenant to the landlord, and may be recovered by the landlord accordingly.

On the order of the Court being made as aforesaid in relation to any holding, all arrears of rent due in respect of that holding on or prior to the gale day next before the passing of this Act, shall be deemed to be absolutely released.

The landlord and tenant may agree that any rent paid by the tenant during the twelve months immediately preceding the passing of this Act shall be deemed, for the purpose of this section, to have been paid in respect of the rent due for the then current year, and not in respect of arrears of rent.

Where arrears of rent in respect of a holding are due to some person or persons besides the landlord, the advance made by the Land Commission under this section shall be rateably distributed by the Court amongst the persons entitled thereto.

An application for an advance under this section shall not be made after the twenty-eighth day of February, one thousand eight hundred and eighty-two.

The omission or refusal by either landlord or tenant of any holding to join with the other of them in obtaining a loan from the Land Commission under this section shall not prejudice any other application or proceeding which either of them may make or institute under this Act, or the Landlord and Tenant (Ireland) Act, 1870, in relation to the holding.

The Land Commission may make advances for the purpose of this section out of any moneys for the time being in their hands for the purposes of this Act.

The Land Commission shall at such time after the expiration of each period of twelve months as the Treasury may from time to time appoint, make up an account showing for the said period of twelve months the amount of all such payments due to them in respect of rentcharges payable to them under this section as they have failed to recover at the expiration of the said period (in this section referred to as payments in arrear), and the Commissioners of Church Temporalities in Ireland shall, out of any moneys at their disposal, pay to the Land Commission any sum appearing from such account to be due to the Land Commission. Any such payment by the Commissioners of Church Temporalities in Ireland shall not discharge any person indebted to the Land Commission in respect of any payments in arrear, and it shall be the duty of the Land Commission to take any proceedings they may be advised for the recovery of payments in arrear, and to repay to the Commissioners of Church Temporalities in Ireland any sums so recovered.

Rules Made by the Irish Land Commission in reference to Advances under the above Section.

115. Where an application is made under Section 59 of the Act, it shall be in Form No. 49, and shall be signed by the landlord or by his agent on his behalf, and by the tenant or tenants who shall concur in such application. It shall moreover be verified by the landlord or his agent, as provided for in such Form, and it shall be forwarded to the Secretary of the Land Commission.

116. If the tenant or any of the tenants concurring in an application under Section 59 of the Act be a tenant or tenants evicted for non-payment of rent since the 1st of May 1880, the application shall, in addition to complying with the requirements mentioned in the preceding Rule, contain an undertaking on the part of the landlord to reinstate such evicted tenant or tenants upon the terms in said Section set forth.

In the case of any application made under the Rules 115 and 116, the Land Commission may call for such information, or direct such further inquiries or evidence, as they may think fit.

FORM No. 60.

LAND LAW (IRELAND) ACT, 1881.

(Section 24.)

Application by Landlord for advances to enable Tenants to purchase their holdings for principal sums.

I   of   in the county of   being

[State whether " owner in fee," " tenant for life," or other " limited owner."]

apply to the Irish Land Commission to make advances to the Tenants named in the first Schedule hereto who have agreed to purchase their holdings for the principal sums set opposite to their names respectively in Column II of said Schedule.

83.   B 3   I have

I have in said first Schedule truly set forth particulars of the said Tenants' holdings respectively.

I have in the second part of the annexed Schedule hereto set forth all the incumbrances to which said holdings are subject, and which it is proposed should be paid off or redeemed out of the purchase-money of said holdings. I believe that the persons in whom the said incumbrances are vested will consent to the sale, and will consent to said incumbrances being paid off or redeemed.

I have in the first part of the said second Schedule set forth all the incumbrances affecting the said holdings which it is not proposed to pay off or redeem, but in respect of which I propose to give an indemnity to the Irish Land Commission, which indemnity I believe to be ample.

The said holdings are not subject to any outgoings save the interest or annual payments in respect of the incumbrances aforesaid, and save the following :—

£ . s . d.

— Lay or Impropriate Tithe.
— Tithe Rentcharge.
— Fixed Instalments in respect of Tithe Rent-charge.—
   These instalments will cease in the year 18 .
— Quit and Crown Rent.
— Head Rent.
— Land Improvement Charge.—This charge will cease in the year 19 .

(State whether it is proposed to redeem any of these outgoings out of the purchase-money. The redemption of them will greatly facilitate the sale.)

The Poor Rates struck for the last five years in the Electoral Division of the Union in which the holdings are situate were as follows :—

For the year, -	187 .	187 .	18 .	18 .	188 .
	s. d.	s. d.	s. d.	s. d.	s. d.
The rate was per £ of valuation					

Dated this   day of   188

(Signature)

(To be signed by the Landlord or by his Agent on his behalf.)

I   of   (the duly appointed Land Agent of

[This affidavit may be made by the Landlord or by his Agent.   If made by the Landlord himself strike out the words in italics.]

, the above-named Landlord, make oath and say as follows:—I have read the above application, and likewise the schedules hereto annexed, and I say that the statements contained in the said application and schedules respectively are true in every particular.

Sworn before me this

[This affidavit may be sworn before a Justice of the Peace or a Commissioner for taking affidavits.]

We, the several Tenants whose names and holdings are set forth in the first Schedule annexed hereto, do hereby join in the above application, and we have signified our assent to it by signing our names opposite to our respective holdings in the column of said Schedule marked L.

Note.—The several columns of figures in the schedules are to be added at foot, and the verification includes the accuracy of the addition as well as of the figures which make it up.
With the application must be sent the sheet or sheets of the 6-inch Ordnance Map, with the several holdings identified or coloured thereon, and marked with numbers to correspond with the numbers of the holdings in the first column of the first Schedule hereto.
The original rentals and accounts for the last five years of the estate on which the holdings are situate must be forwarded to the Land Commission for examination if required.
The tenants on each townland should be placed on separate Schedules if necessary.
All applications must be in duplicate.

FIRST SCHEDULE.

County _____ . Barony of _____ . Poor Law Union _____ .

Electoral Division _____ . Name of Townland, as known on) _____
　　　　　　　　　　　　　　　　　　　Ordnance Survey Map -)

Left hand.

Marks for Reading to the left Blank.	A Number of Holding to correspond with the Number on the Ordnance Map and herewith.	B Name of the Tenant.	C Tenure of Present.	D Gale Days.	E Area of Holding, Statute Measure.	F Gross Poor Law Valuation.	G Tenant's Rent.
					A. R. P.	£ s. d.	£ s. d.

Right hand.

H Principal Sum agreed to be Paid for the Holding.	I Amount of Advance applied for from Irish Land Commission.	K How the Balance is proposed to be made up, whether by Cash Payment or by Mortgage to Landlord.	L Signature of Tenant.	M Witness to Signature of Tenant.	Observations.
£ s. d.	£ s. d.				

For Second Schedule, see page 43.

LAND LAW (IRELAND) ACT, 1881.

Contract by Landlord to Sell to Tenants through the medium of the Irish Land Commission, in consideration of a Principal Sum.

By this Contract, dated the   day of   188 . and made between the within-named   hereinafter called " the Landlord," and the several persons named in the First Schedule hereto, hereinafter called " the Tenants," the Landlord agrees to sell and the Tenants to purchase, through the medium of the Irish Land Commission, the several holdings set opposite to the names of the Tenants respectively in column E of said Schedule, for the price set opposite to their names respectively in column H of said Schedule.

And it is hereby agreed and declared that the outgoings to which the estate is liable as set forth in the within application, shall be apportioned among the Tenants in the proportions set forth in the Memorandum hereunder written.

[This paragraph may be struck out if it is not proposed to apportion the outgoings among the Tenants purchasing.]

In witness whereof the Landlord has hereunto subscribed his name, and the Tenants have in column L of said Schedule subscribed their names.

Signed by the Landlord in }
     presence of   -   -   - }

Name, }
Address, } of Witness {
Description, }

MEMORANDUM ABOVE REFERRED TO.

FORM No. 51.

LAND LAW (IRELAND) ACT, 1881.

Application by Landlord for Advances to enable Tenants to purchase their Holdings for a Fine and Fee-farm Rent.

I   of   in the county of   , being

[State whether " owner in fee," " tenant for life," or other " limited owner."]

apply to the Irish Land Commission to make advances to the Tenants named in the first Schedule hereto who have agreed to purchase their holdings in consideration of the fines and fee-farm rents set opposite to their names respectively in column H of said Schedule.

I have in said first Schedule truly set forth particulars of the said Tenants' holdings respectively.

I have in the first part of the said second Schedule set forth all the incumbrances affecting the said holdings which it is not proposed to pay off or redeem, but in respect of which I propose to give an indemnity to the Irish Land Commission, which indemnity I believe to be ample.

I have in the second part of the second Schedule hereto set forth all the incumbrances to which said holdings are subject, and which it is proposed should be paid off or redeemed out of the purchase money of said holdings.

I believe that the persons in whom the said incumbrances are vested will consent to the sale, and will consent to said incumbrances being paid off or redeemed.

The

The said holdings are not subject to any outgoings save the interest or annual payments in respect of the incumbrances aforesaid, and save the following :—

£.	s.	d.	
			—Lay or Impropriate Tithes.
			—Tithe Rentcharge.
			—Fixed Instalments in respect of Tithe Rentcharge.— These instalments will cease in the year 18 .
			—Quit and Crown Rent.
			—Head Rent.
			—Land Improvement Charge.—This charge will cease in the year 18 .

[State whether it is proposed to redeem any of these outgoings out of the purchase money. The redemption of these will greatly facilitate the sale.]

The Poor Rates struck for the last five years in the Electoral Division of the Union in which the holdings are situate, were as follows :—

For the year	.	187	187	18	18	188	.
The rate was per £. of valuation,	.	s. d.	s. d.	s. d.	s. d.	s. d.	

Dated this   day of   188

(Signature)

[To be signed by the Landlord or by his Agent on his behalf.]

I   of   (the duly appointed Land Agent of   ), the above-named Landlord, make oath and say as

[This affidavit may be made by the Landlord or by his Agent. If made by the Landlord himself strike out the words in italics.]

follows :—I have read the above application, and likewise the schedules hereto annexed, and I say that the statements contained in the said application and schedules respectively are true in every particular.

Sworn before me this

[This affidavit may be sworn before a Justice of the Peace or a Commissioner for taking affidavits.]

We, the several Tenants whose names and holdings are set forth in the First Schedule annexed hereto, do hereby join in the above Application, and we have signified our assent to it by signing our names opposite to our respective holdings in the column of said Schedule marked L.

Note.—The several columns of figures in the schedules are to be added as flat, and the verification includes the accuracy of the addition as well as of the figures which make it up.

With the application must be sent the above or a copy of the 6-inch Ordnance Map, with the several holdings sketched or coloured thereon, and marked with numbers to correspond with the numbers of the holdings in the first column of the first schedule hereto.

The original rentals and accounts for the last five years of the estate on which the holdings are situate must be forwarded to the Land Commission for examination if required.

The tenancies on each townland should be placed on separate schedules if numerous.

All applications must be in duplicate.

FIRST SCHEDULE.

County_____   Barony of_____   Poor Law Union_____
Electoral Division_____   Name of Townland, as known on ⎫_____
Ordnance Survey Map - ⎭

Left hand.

Margin for Binding to the last Blank.	A Number of Holding to correspond with the Number on the Ordnance Map and herewith.	B Name of Tenant.	C Tenure of Tenant.	D Gale Days.	E Area of Holding, Statute Measure.	F Gross Poor Law Valuation.	G Tenant's Rent.
					A. R. P.	£. s. d.	£. s. d.

Right hand.

H Term of Holding.		I Amount of Advance Applied for from Irish Land Commission.	K How the Balance is proposed to be made up, whether by Cash Payment or by Mortgage to Landlord.	L Signature of Tenant.	M Witness to Signature of Tenant.	Observations.
Plan.	Fee-Farm Rent.					
£. s. d.	£. s. d.	£. s. d.				

For Second Schedule, see page 43.

LAND LAW (IRELAND) ACT, 1891.

Contract by Landlord to sell to Tenants through the medium of the Irish Land Commission, in consideration of a Fine and a Fee-form Rent.

By this Contract, dated the _____ day of _____, 189 , and made between the within-named _____ , hereinafter called "The Landlord," and the several persons named in the First Schedule hereto, hereinafter called "The Tenants," the Landlord agrees to sell and the Tenants to purchase, through the medium of the Irish Land Commission, the several holdings set opposite to the names of the Tenants respectively in column E of said Schedule, for the price set opposite to their names respectively in column H of said Schedule.

And it is hereby agreed and declared that the outgoings to which the estate is liable, as set forth in the within application, shall be apportioned among the Tenants in the proportions set forth in the Memorandum hereunder written.

[This paragraph may be struck out if it is not proposed to apportion the outgoings among the Tenants purchasing.]

In witness whereof the Landlord has hereunto subscribed his name, and the Tenants have in column L of said Schedule subscribed their names.

Signed by the Landlord in }
    presence of }

Name, }
Address, } of Witness {
Description, }

MEMORANDUM ABOVE REFERRED TO.

LAND LAW (IRELAND) ACT, 1891.

Advances to enable Tenants to purchase from Landlord.

SECOND SCHEDULE.

To be annexed to Applications 50, 51, or 53.

County of _____ . Barony of _____ Poor Law Union of _____
Electoral Division of _____ Townland of _____
Name of Landlord _____ Address of Landlord _____

Name and Address of Agent, if any, to whom Communications } _____
    on the subject of the Application are to be addressed } _____

This is the Second Schedule to my Application this day verified by me.

Dated _____ day of _____ 18 .

_____
Land Agent of _____

_____

* The party verifying the Application should sign here.
† The Justice of the Peace or Commissioner before whom the Application is verified should sign here.

County _____ Barony _____ Poor Law Union _____
Electoral Division _____ Name of Townland _____

63.　　　　F 2

SECOND SCHEDULE.

First Part, showing Incumbrances not proposed to be paid off, but in respect of which an Indemnity will be given.

Left hand.

Date of Incumbrance.	Name of Party entitled thereto.	Address of Party entitled thereto.	Manner in which Charge was created.	Sum Due for Principal.
				£ s. d.

Right hand.

Annual Rate of Interest.	Days of Payment of Interest or Annuity.	Amount Due for Interest or Arrears of Annuity.	Gale Day on which Interest or Arrears of Annuity are Due.	Special Circumstances relating to each Incumbrance.
		£ s. d.		

County of _____   Barony of _____   Poor Law Union of _____

Electoral Division of _____   Townland of _____

SECOND SCHEDULE.

Second Part, showing Incumbrances proposed to be paid off out of the Purchase Money.

Left hand.

Date of Incumbrance.	Name of Party entitled thereto.	Address of Party entitled thereto.	Manner in which Charge was created.	Sum Due for Principal.
				£ s. d.

Right hand.

Annual Rate of Interest.	Days of Payment of Interest.	Amount Due for Interest or Arrears of Annuity.	Gale Day on which Interest or Arrears of Annuity are Due.	Special Circumstances relating to each Incumbrance.
		£ s. d.		

Form No. 62.

LAND LAW (IRELAND) ACT, 1881.

Application to Irish Land Commission to negotiate a Sale from Landlord to Tenants under Section 24.

County_____   Barony_____

Poor Law Union_____   Electoral Division_____

Townland, as known on Ordnance Survey Map_____

Other name of Townland (if any)_____

Name of Landlord_____   Address of Landlord_____

Name and Address of Tenant or other person to whom communications should be addressed on behalf of the Tenants of the Estate. }_____

I, _____, the Landlord of the above-named Estate, apply to the Irish Land Commission to negotiate the sale of said Estate to the Tenants thereof, and I undertake to pay for the expenses of such negotiation, and of the completion of each sale, according to the following scale, that is to say—

	£ s. d.
For the expenses of negotiation, up to and including signing of the contract, on every 100 £ of the purchase money - - - - - - - - -	- 10 -
For subsequent expenses, including (if contract be completed) Conveyance from me to the Tenants, Mortgage to the Commission, Registration, and Stamp Duty on every 100 £ of the purchase money - - -	1 - -

Dated   day of   18

Signed,

[To be signed by the Landlord.]

We, the undersigned Tenants on the above-named Estate, concur in the above application.

Signed,

[To be signed by the Tenants of the Estate, or some of them, if they concur in the application.]

Form No. 63.

LAND LAW (IRELAND) ACT, 1881.

Application by Landlord to sell an Estate under Section 26.

I   of   in the county of   being

[State whether "owner in fee," "tenant for life," or other "limited owner."]

of the lands described in the first Schedule hereto, propose to sell the said lands as an estate to the Irish Land Commission, in pursuance of Section 26 of the Land Law (Ireland) Act, 1881.

I believe that a competent number of tenants, being not less than three-fourths of the whole number of Tenants on the estate, and paying not less than two-thirds of the rental, are able and willing to purchase their holdings.

83.   F 3   The

The Tenants who are, as I believe, able and willing to purchase their holdings for a "principal sum," are those numbered in said Schedule from 1 to   , both inclusive.

The Tenants who are, as I believe, able and willing to purchase their holdings, in consideration of a fine, and a fee-farm rent, are numbered in said Schedule from to   , both inclusive.

The Tenants who, as I believe, are not able or willing to purchase their holdings, are numbered in said Schedule from   to   , both inclusive.

I have in said first Schedule truly set forth particulars of the said Tenants' holdings respectively.

I have in the first part of the annexed Schedule set forth all the incumbrances affecting said holdings which it is not proposed to pay off or redeem, but in respect of which I propose to give an indemnity to the Irish Land Commission, and which indemnity I believe to be ample.

I have in the second part of the annexed Schedule hereto set forth all the incumbrances to which said lands are subject, and which it is proposed should be paid off or redeemed out of the purchase money of said lands. I believe that the persons in whom said incumbrances are vested will consent to the sale, and will consent to said incumbrances being paid off or redeemed.

The said lands are not subject to any outgoings save the interest or annual payments in respect of the incumbrances aforesaid, and save the following :—

Amount of Outgoings.	Nature of Outgoings.[a]
£. s. d.	
	Lay or Impropriate Tithes.
	Tithe Rentcharge.
	Fixed Instalments in lieu of Tithe Rentcharge. These will come in the year
	Quit and Crown Rent.
	Land Improvement Charges. These will cease in the year
	Head Rent.
	Total Outgoings.

[a State whether it is proposed to redeem any of these outgoings out of the purchase money. The redemption of them will greatly facilitate the carrying out of the proposed sale.]

The Poor Rates struck for the last five years in the Electoral Division of the Union in which the holdings are situate, were as follows :—

For the year	187 .	187 .	18 .	18 .	189 .
	s. d.	s. d.	s. d.	s. d.	s. d.
The rate was per £ of valuation.					

Dated this   day of   188 .

(Signature),

[To be signed by the Landlord or by his Agent on his behalf.]

[of (the duly appointed Land Agent of

[This affidavit may be made by the Landlord or his Agent. If made by the Landlord himself strike out the words in italics.]

, the above named Landlord, make oath and say as follows:—I have read the above application, and likewise the schedules hereto annexed, and I say that the statements contained in the said application and schedules respectively are true in every particular.

Sworn before me this

[This affidavit may be sworn before a Justice of the Peace, or a Commissioner for taking affidavits.]

Note.—The several columns of figures in the schedules are to be added at foot, and the verification includes the accuracy of the addition as well as of the figures which make it up.

With the application must be sent the plan or sheet of the 6-inch Ordnance Map, with the several holdings sketched or coloured thereon, and marked with numbers to correspond with the numbers of the holdings in the first column of the first schedule hereto.

The original rentals and accounts for the last five years of the estate on which the holdings are situate must be forwarded to the Land Commission for examination if required.

The tenancies on each townland should be placed on separate schedules if necessary.

All applications must be in duplicate.

Note.—Firstly—Set out the Tenants able and willing to purchase for a principal sum, and add their rents at foot.

Secondly—Set out the Tenants able and willing to purchase their holdings in consideration of a fine and fee-farm rent, and add their rents at foot.

Thirdly—Set out the Tenants not able or willing to purchase, and add their rents at foot.

FIRST SCHEDULE.

County.   Barony of ____   Poor Law Union

Electoral Division   Name of Townland, as known on Ordnance Survey Map   Other Name, if any

Left hand.

Margin for Binding up in the left blank.	A Number of Holding to correspond with the Number on the Ordnance Map.	B Name of the Tenant.	C Tenure of Tenant.	D Gale Days.	E Area of Holding, Statute Measure.
					A. R. P.

Right hand.

F Gross Poor Law Valuation.	G Tenant's Rent.	H	I	OBSERVATIONS.
£ s. d.	£ s. d.	£ s. d.	£ s. d.	

For Second Schedule, see page 48.

FORM No. 54.

LAND LAW (IRELAND) ACT, 1881.

Proposal by Landlord to sell an Estate under Section 26, and Undertaking to
Pay Expenses.

County_____   Barony .

Poor Law Union__ _____   Electoral Division _____ _

Townland, as known on Ordnance Survey Map ___ _____

Other name of Townland (if any) __ __ __

Name of Landlord_____   Address of Landlord_____

I,   , the above-named Landlord, do hereby propose to sell to the
Irish Land Commission, for the sum of £. , the above-named Lands, the particulars of which are set forth in the application made by me to the Irish Land Commission,
dated the day of , 18 , and I undertake to pay to the
Irish Land Commission, for the expenses of such Sale, according to the following scale,
that is to say :—

                                                 £. s. d.

For the expenses up to and including notice by the Commission to the Landlord of their being willing to
purchase - - - - - - - - - - 10 - per 100 l.

Together with the subsequent expenses, that is to say, the actual outlay by the Commission in completing the sale.

Signed by me this   day of   , 18 .

                             Signature of Landlord_____

Signed by the said Landlord in
presence of

         Signature }
         Address   } of Witness.
         Description }

FORM No. 55.

LAND LAW (IRELAND) ACT, 1881.

Undertaking by Tenants to Purchase their Holdings under Section 26.

County_____   Barony _

Poor Law Union . _____   Electoral Division_____

Townland, as known on Ordnance Survey Map. ___ _____

Other name (if any)_ __ __ . . .

Landlord_____

Name and Address of Person to whom communications are to be addressed on behalf
of the Tenants.

We, the Tenants named in the First Schedule hereto, do hereby undertake to purchase
from the Irish Land Commission the holdings set opposite to our names respectively in
column C of said Schedule, at the prices named in column E thereof, in witness whereof
we have signed our names respectively in column F of said Schedule;
                        and

We, the Tenants named in the Second Schedule hereto, do hereby undertake to
purchase from the Irish Land Commission the holdings set opposite to our names
respectively in column C of said Schedule, at the prices named in column E thereof.
In witness whereof we have signed our names respectively in column F of said
Schedule.

            Dated this   day of   188

FIRST SCHEDULE.

Showing the Holdings, the Tenants of which agree to Purchase *for a Principal Sum.*

A	B	C	D	E	F	G
Number of Holding to correspond with the Number on the Ordnance Map.	Name of Tenant.	Area of Holding in Statute Measure.	Tenant's Rent.	Price at which Tenants agree to Purchase their Holdings.	Signature of Tenant.	Name, Address, and Description of Witness to Tenant's Signature.
		A. R. P.	£ s. d.	£ s. d.		

SECOND SCHEDULE.

Showing the Holdings, the Tenants of which agree to Purchase on Condition of a Fine and a Fee-farm Rent.

A	B	C	D	E		F	G
Number of Holding to correspond with the Number on the Ordnance Map.	Name of Tenant.	Area of Holding in Statute Measure.	Tenant's Rent.	Price at which Tenants Agree to Purchase their Holdings.		Signature of Tenant.	Name, Address, and Description of Witness to Tenant's Signature.
				Amount of Fine.	Fee-farm Rent.		
		A. R. P.	£ s. d.	£ s. d.	£ s. d.		

FORM No. 54.

LAND LAW (IRELAND) ACT, 1881.

Application by Tenants to the Irish Land Commission to purchase an Estate for Sale in the Court of the Land Judges.

In the Matter of the Estate of
County of

Owner }
Petitioner.

We, the undersigned, being Tenants on Lot of the above-named Estate, apply to the Irish Land Commission to purchase said Lot.

A copy of the rental (or Consolidated Final Notice to Tenants) is sent herewith.

[*Note.*—In case the Rental has been settled, a copy of such Rental must be sent with this application; and if the Rental has not been settled, a copy of the Consolidated Final Notice to Tenants must be sent.]

We undertake to abide by any order the Land Commission may make for the purpose of protecting the Commission against loss on such purchase.

Dated this   day of   188

Signed,

(The Land Commission cannot purchase any Lot unless three-fourths of the Tenants paying not less than two-thirds of the rental are able and willing to purchase their holdings.)

Name and Address of person to whom { Name ——————
communications are to be addressed { Address ——————
on behalf on the Tenants. { Post Town ——————

FORM No. 57.

[Heading same as Form No. 1.]

Submission to Arbitration.

The Landlord and Tenant do hereby refer the dispute between them as to
[State specifically nature of dispute.]

to the arbitration and award of
[Name, residence, and description of Arbitrators.]

And in case of difference between them to the umpirage of
abide by the arbitration of, or umpirage as the case may be, when
[Name, residence, and description of umpire.]

and agree to

Signed,

Signed,

[To be signed by the Landlord or his Agent, and by the Tenant.]

To_____

Seal of
the Irish Land
Commission.

John O'Hagan,
B. F. Litton,
John E. Vernon.

COURT FEES.

	£.	s.	d.
Every originating notice served after the date of these Rules, and every notice of appeal shall bear an impressed stamp of · · | | - | 1 | - |

[No other Court Fees shall be payable in proceedings under the
Act in the Court of the Land Commission, or in the Civil Bill
Courts, until the 31st March 1883.]

SOLICITORS' FEES.

1. In all proceedings under the Act the fees specified in the schedule to these Rules annexed, shall be the lawful fees and emoluments for the discharge of the duties therein specified by solicitors. And, subject to the powers by the Act, or hereinafter given to the Court, no other fees or emoluments shall be recoverable for the discharge of such duties, or be allowed in any bill of costs, between party and party, or (in the absence of special agreement) between solicitor and client. They shall be taxable in the Court of the Land Commission by the Registrar, or by any Sub-Commission, and in the Civil Bill Court by the Clerk of the Peace, his Deputy, or principal Assistant.

2. The fees specified shall include all outlay except postage, Court fees, fees for service, fees to counsel, and expenses of process servers and witnesses.

3. The Court in all cases shall have power, when a solicitor is specially employed outside the district where he usually practises, or under other special circumstances, to increase the fees allowed to the solicitor for any party beyond the amount specified in the schedule, and this either as between party and party, or as between solicitor and client, or both.

4. Where

4. Where two or more cases, involving similar questions, and arising with respect to holdings held under the same landlord, are heard at the same place and sittings, and have been consolidated by the Court, the Court shall have power to award to the solicitor or solicitors conducting the same a bulk sum for his costs in respect of all the cases in which he so appears, and, if necessary, to settle the proportions in which the same shall be borne and received respectively.

5. The Court shall have power to give or withhold the costs either in the whole or in part of any proceedings under this Act, and to direct the same or any portion thereof, to be paid by the opposite party and generally to make such orders with reference to the payment of costs as having regard to the circumstances of any case is shall deem meet.

6. The costs on appeal before the Land Commission shall follow the same scale, but subject to be increased by the Court where the appeal is not heard in the same county in which the case was heard below.

7. The schedule of fees hereby settled is intended to be the remuneration for all business done as well before as after the case is opened in Court. If the case be not opened in Court one-half only of the specified fees shall be allowed.

SCHEDULE OF FEES.

SALE OF TENANCIES.

	£.	s.	d.
For all proceedings consequent on a tenant's notice of his intention to sell his tenancy where an originating notice is served, from the first originating notice up to and including the payment and distribution of the purchase-money.			
Where the rent of the holding mentioned in the tenant's notice of intention to sell does not exceed 5 *l.*	1	—	—
Where such rent exceeds 5 *l.* and does not exceed 15 *l.*	2	—	—
Where such rent exceeds 15 *l.* and is under 50 *l.*	3	—	—
Where rent exceeds 50 *l.*	5	—	—

The above scale shall likewise apply:

1. In case of sale by an execution creditor, assignee in bankruptcy, personal representative, or other person selling the tenancy:

2. Where the landlord makes application to the Court to sell the tenancy, by reason of the default of the personal representative to nominate a successor to the tenancy or sell.

Whenever the landlord or tenant makes application to the Court to ascertain the depreciation in the selling value of a tenancy consequent on an increase of rent.			
For all proceedings from the originating notice to the final order of the Court.			
If the rent stated in the notice of application do not exceed 50 *l.*	1	—	—
If it exceed 50 *l.*	2	—	—
In case of an application by the landlord for resumption of the holding or part thereof under Section 5 of the Act. For all proceedings from the originating notice to the final order of the Court.			
If the rent stated in the originating notice do not exceed 50 *l.*	1	—	—
If it exceed 50 *l.*	2	—	—

FAIR RENT.

Where application is made to fix a fair rent.

For all proceedings from the originating notice to the final order of the Court.

	£	s.	d.
Where the rent stated in the originating notice do not exceed 5 l.	—	10	—
Where it exceeds 5 l. but does not exceed 15 l.	1	—	—
Where it exceeds 15 l. but does not exceed 50 l.	2	—	—
Where it exceeds 50 l. but does not exceed 100 l.	3	—	—
Where it exceeds 100 l.	4	—	—

In cases of agreement fixing the fair rent of holdings.

For all proceedings from the preparation of the agreement and declaration fixing the fair rent, to the obtaining the certificate of the filing thereof.

	£	s.	d.
If the rent stated in the agreement do not exceed 5 l.	—	5	—
If it exceeds 5 l. but does not exceed 15 l.	—	10	—
If it exceeds 15 l. but do not exceed 50 l.	1	—	—
If it exceeds 50 l.	2	—	—

Judicial Leases and Fixed Tenancies.

To the solicitor preparing a judicial lease, for preparing and furnishing the draft lease, obtaining the approbation thereof by the Court, engrossing the lease and counterpart, and obtaining the execution of same by all necessary parties, and the signing by the County Court Judge, or the Secretary of the Land Commission, and all things incidental to the above matters (except the stamp duty on the lease and counterpart, Court fees, fees to counsel, and postage):

	£	s.	d.
If the rent, subject to which the lease is made, do not exceed 5 l.	1	—	—
If it exceed 5 l. and do not exceed 30 l.	2	—	—
If it exceed 30 l.	3	—	—

If a solicitor be employed by the opposite party—to such solicitor for approving of draft lease and attending in Court to consent when ever necessary, half the foregoing fees.

For preparing the agreement to create a fixed tenancy (where the approval of the Court is required) and all subsequent proceedings, up to and including the execution and approval of the grant.

The same fees as in the case of a judicial lease.

PROCEEDINGS UNDER PART IV. OF THE ACT.

The following shall be the scale of fees where rent stated in Notice of Application exceeds 5 l. and does not exceed 50 l.:—When the rent does not exceed 5 l. the fees shall be one-half, and when the rent exceeds 50 l. the fees shall be double of the following.

In case of application by a tenant to restrain proceedings under a notice to quit.

	£	s.	d.
To the tenant's solicitor for preparing the affidavit to grant the application, settling the originating notice, and also for the proceedings down to the final order of the Court	1	—	—
To landlord's solicitor if the application be resisted	1	—	—

In case of application by tenant to let portion of a holding for the use of labourers.

For all proceedings from the originating notice to the final order of the Court.

	£	s.	d.
To the tenant's solicitor	-	10	-
To the landlord's solicitor if the application be resisted	-	10	-

In case of an application by the landlord for the resumption of a holding under section 21 of the Act.

For all proceedings from the originating notice to the final order of the Court.

To the solicitors of the landlord and tenant respectively.

If the rent stated in the originating notice do not exceed 30l.	-	10	-
If it exceed 30l.	1	-	-

In the case of an application to have a lease accepted since 1st August 1870, declared void.

For all proceedings from the originating notice to the final order of the Land Commission.

To the respective solicitors of the landlord and tenant	2	-	-

Where Counsel is employed.

Instructions for counsel's brief, and attending counsel, where rent is over 5l. and under 50l.	-	6	8
Brief of documents for each sheet of six folios	-	1	-

Counsel's Fees.

Where rent of holding is under 30l.	1	1	-
Where rent exceeds 30l.	2	2	-

But counsel's fees shall in no case be allowed against the opposite party unless certified for by the Court.

(Seal of the Irish Land Commission.)

John O'Hagan,
E. F. Litton,
John E. Vernon.

24, Upper Merrion-street, Dublin.

Denis Godley.

LAND LAW (IRELAND) ACT, 1881
(RULES, FORMS, &c.).

COPY of RULES, FORMS, and SCHEDULE of FEES
Issued by the IRISH LAND COMMISSION.

(*Presented pursuant to Act of Parliament.*)

Ordered, by The House of Commons, to be Printed,
8 March 1882.

[*Price 7 d.*]

83.

E—R.A.V.   *Under 8 oz.*

www.ingramcontent.com/pod-product-compliance
Lightning Source LLC
Chambersburg PA
CBHW021642270326
41931CB00008B/1124